the
millennium
city
Hermit

Anuj Bajaj

Copyright © 2016 by Anuj Bajaj

All rights reserved. This book or any portion thereof may not be reproduced or used in any manner whatsoever without the express written permission of the publisher except for the use of brief quotations in a book review.

Some names and identifying details have been changed to protect the privacy of individuals.

First Printing, 2016
Printed in India
Printed by: Dhote Offset Printers

ISBN : 978-93-83952-90-8

Editing: Wordit CDE
Cover Design: Rahul Saini
Marketed By - Nishkaam Nishtha
436, Plot no. 6, Tower Lane, Rangpuri Extension,
Westendgreen farm house barrier
Email Id - nishkaamnishtha@gmail.com
Contact no - +919818331010

The Write Place
A Publishing Initiative by Crossword Bookstores Ltd.
Paradigm, A-Wing, 1st Floor, Mindspace, Link Road,
Malad West, Mumbai 400064, India.

Web: www.TheWritePlace.in
Facebook: TheWritePlace.in
Twitter: @WritePlacePub
Instagram: @WritePlacePub

GRATITUDE

As an instrument to this compilation, I have read it multiple times before the print. Every time I read it, I could not gather the courage to give myself the credit for writing it. It was the discipline that prevented any kind of dilution of content, that took its origin in the Self. The flow of thoughts was like a smooth stream, the *Buddhi* (Mind) contemplated and delved effortlessly, the fingers manifested the un-manifested, without any attachment to fruit.

The Divinity is the energy behind all manifestation. I respect the sanctity of the flow of thoughts and wish the continuance of the discipline and blessings of the Almighty.

Gratitude to friends and family for their support.

Inspirations, Insights and Critics – Works of Dr. H.R Nagendra of S-VYASA Institute and Swami Rama, Library friend Gyan Yogi Mr. Vijender Singh, Karm Yogi Mr. Arjun Vir Bajaj, Mother Mrs. Alka Bajaj, Master in Yoga Sc. Ms. Neha Bajaj, brothers Mr. Ranjan Malik & Mr. Amit Bajaj and morning walk partner Mr. Ajay Batra.

Cover Page – Illustration taken from a series of paintings of Mr. R.K Saini - 'Aura'. Cover page design done by Mr. Rahul Saini - Design Head, Paytm.

Editors at various stages – Mr. Arjun Bajaj, Ms. Neha Bajaj, Ms. Anusha Malhotra and the Wordit team.

CONTENTS

	Page No.
Chapter 1 : An Unplanned Beginning	5
Chapter 2 : It's All In Our Hands	11
Chapter 3 : Gita – The Key To Happy Living	16
Chapter 4 : Trigunas: A Success Mantra	23
Chapter 5 : The Urdu Manuscript	27
Chapter 6 : Trigunas – The Concept	34
Chapter 7 : Duty And Attachment	38
Chapter 8 : Sequential Progression Of Trigunas	51
Chapter 9 : Tilling And Nurturing	61
Chapter 10 : Internal Discipline	71
Chapter 11 : External Discipline	80
Chapter 12 : Amitabh Bachchan – A Case Study	91
Chapter 13 : Kumbh *Mela*	104
Chapter 14 : Mind	113
Chapter 15 : Disciplines That Make Buddhi Strong	124
Chapter 16 : Freedom, Creativity And Sattva	136
Chapter 17 : Word Of Caution	145
Chapter 18 : Parting Words	160
Chapter 19 : Himaayat Ali	168
Author's Note	177
Research Work	180

CHAPTER ONE

AN UNPLANNED BEGINNING

Surprised by the knowledge of the naked Naga Sadhu I realised there is more to it than meets the eye.

In the enthusiasm of finally being able to visit the Kumbh *Mela*, I had booked my tickets early, so as to be a part of the most 'auspicious' day of the *Mela*, 10th of February and here I was. The 40-Day Kumbh *Mela* was reaching its peak and the wee hours of February 10 were the 'auspicious' hours when a dip in the Ganges could give you a direct entry into heaven.

Kumbh *Mela* is the largest congregation of religious people in the world. The *Sangam* point or *Triveni* of Allahabad hosts the Kumbh *Mela* once every 12 years while the *Mela* is held at various other points on the banks of Ganges every 4 years. More than 120 million people were expected to visit this 40-Day *Mela* that year. On the auspicious bathing dates more than 20 million devotees take a dip in the holy waters of Ganga within 24 hours. People from around the world come to analyse various aspects of the Kumbh *Mela*.

The whole *Mela* is organised in a temporary structure on the banks of the river. More than 35 thousand temporary toilets are built for 40 days. 14 temporary hospitals are built and 30,000 policemen are engaged to ensure safety of the devotees. All arrangements are made just for 40 days. There are no concrete structures – after 40 days the *Mela* area reverts to a piece of barren land on the banks of the Ganges.

On this day – February 10 – there were more than 25 million devotees who took a dip in the Holy Ganga – the highest number of dips in the *Triveni Sangam* on a single day!

Early this morning, I had bought three packs of Wills Navy Cut cigarettes; I knew this would be the key to having a conversation with the *Naga Sadhus* – the sect of devotees indulged in smoking as a ritual. They are devotees of Shiva and they smoke the naturally rolled marijuana obtained from plants in the mountains. The *Naga* sect is supposed to be comprised of warriors and were formed as the protectors of Hinduism against the rule of the Islamic Mughals.

Naga Sadhus are the most celebrated participants of the Kumbh *Mela*. These *Sadhus* have renounced the materialistic world. They are essentially naked *sadhus* who follow the ritual of rubbing ash on their body to signify that their material self has been cremated and that they now live a life of complete detachment. Kumbh *Mela* is the only occasion when they descend from their hermitage in the Himalayas and spend 40 days among other people. The bare bodied *sadhus* smoking their chillums are the most photographed cults in the Kumbh.

So here I was, smoking a Wills Navy Cut with a young Naga Sadhu. We were engaged in a meaningful conversation when suddenly my phone rang. As I took out my mobile phone from my pocket, to my surprise the Naga Sadhu exclaimed, "Ah, Samsung Galaxy Note." This knowledge of trending gadgets from a renunciant who had just descended from the mountains was unexpected.

I was curious about how, and when did these worldly human beings take the plunge to renounce the world. What was their pursuit in doing so? Have they actually no desires or are they suppressing their desires? My inquisitiveness made me look for a *sadhu* who would be willing to divulge more and I trusted the cigarettes to buy time.

As I walked around and conversed with a few of them, I finally encountered a more forthcoming Naga Sadhu. He spoke of their routine in the *ashram* and admitted to no knowledge of the scriptures. He said that when he was younger, he used to run a shop selling spectacles. He'd even tried to join the Army. His friend becoming a Naga Sadhu was the only explanation he could give about him becoming a Naga Sadhu too.

This got me thinking as to what was I doing here?

It was an unplanned beginning for me too. I had worked in corporate jobs for three years and then got a business opportunity in the newly privatised telecom industry in India. I ran a flourishing business for six years that made handsome returns. But as with all new industries, the telecom business also saw some rectification and the returns dipped at par with any other industry. Although still growing, there was an inherent desire to move on from a franchisee-based business to building a brand.

Living in a joint family does make one take some wise decisions. Together with my brother and father we invested in a commercial space. Soon, we started a 48-seater restaurant with a small 50 pax banqueting facility.

In retrospect, I thank god for having designed the path he designed for me in this life. The restaurant was the third establishment to open in the newly constructed market. It started to sustain itself within a year and was getting my full attention from day one. I gave up the franchisee business to run the restaurant. However, my lifestyle and routine went for a toss with corporate catering in the morning to banquet parties in the evening.

My day would start at 9 am with corporate catering, followed by busy lunch hours in the restaurant and then evening banquets. Weekends were busy, festivals were busier. Family life took a back seat and lack of exercise made things worse. The business started giving returns but was not matching up to the previous income levels that I had got used to. From 3 pm to 5 pm I would go home only to come back for supervising the arrangements for the banquets; the day would finally get over at 11 pm.

The business had not reached a stage where it could afford professional managers. And I belonged to a service class background where operating losses were not acceptable. Soon I realised that I was not meant to live a lifestyle like that. The last straw broke when we took up the bar license – the bar required my attention late into the night.

Personally, I had always enjoyed social outings to the bar with friends. Often, we would become irritant to the staff for ordering another peg after the last order. But now the tables had turned; I was part of the staff that got irritated by guests who wanted to be served beyond the closing time.

And before I knew it, all that meticulous planning was leading to an unplanned decision. I was organising a gala evening for a New Year party at the banquet. 31st of December – New Year's Eve – is the highest grosser for the Food and Beverage industry across the world. Owners personally get involved in the minutiae to ensure that the best is delivered. Even our vendor for special bakery breads came personally to deliver the order.

This baker, who was in his sixties, with a short pony tail and a salt and pepper beard, had a good sense of humour. As a warm gesture, I walked out to see him off. As we were parting he asked me how life was and what my plans were in the New Year. I genuinely replied, "I hope to change my lifestyle in the New Year to a more healthy and peaceful one."

He gave me a smile as he sat in his car and politely replied, "Son, look back into the past and then into the future, is it not what you resolved last year and last to last year and the year before." He smiled as we parted and said, "Have a lot of bread to sell tonight. All the best, son."

I still thank him for reiterating the obvious. After all, *if you do the same thing, you will get the same result*. And so I made my unplanned move. By January 5, I stopped going to the restaurant. I organised the management of the restaurant from home. I resumed my life, started going for a morning jog, took my kids to the park in the evening. Just one week into this new lifestyle made me bolder. I took a call and started contacting other restaurant owners with an offer to take over the running restaurant and bar on rent. From the 1st of April, I was a free man.

**If you do the same thing,
you will get the same result.**

CHAPTER TWO

IT'S ALL IN OUR HANDS

My father is a bold man, a visionary and a hard taskmaster. When he was 41, he was hired by a healthcare company to launch a pharmaceutical division; he launched the pharma division from scratch. He used to carry some of his ideas home. These ideas sparked a lot of healthy discussions. We used to discuss names of new products, market competition, etc. In three years, the division had reached an enviable position and was acknowledged as a valued profit center. He then realised it was time to launch himself as an entrepreneur and quit his job at 49. At the time, my elder brother was barely out of college, and my mother was teaching in a school. All set to put his best foot forward, he convinced my mother to give up her job and the three of them started a logistics company. After a few years of immense hard work and struggle, their efforts were met with success. Thanks to all three of them I had an alternative office to go to now. Soon, I was in the logistics business.

After more than a decade of handling the telecom and restaurant business single handedly, it was a comfortable change to be in business with my brother. Father and mother had retired to homely pursuits. Father rendered his guidance to us from the comfort of home; they enjoyed their frequent travel and time with the grandchildren.

At the logistics business front, healthy discussions between my brother and myself and effective implementation reached logical conclusions. Together, we soon steered our company to touch new heights.

Three years of the restaurant business had left my mind deluded. Dedicated work and a keen eye on returns (wealth creation) was a lifestyle that I had led with passion. I was self-employed since a decade now and the result of my action had a direct impact on my lifestyle, as with most entrepreneurs. The three years in the restaurant business were financial low points for me. But the life that I had led in those three years had helped me evolve as a person. As I got back into a regular office routine, I found more time to myself to contemplate the larger meaning of life and my existence.

I realised that what I am doing, as a bread earner, is my duty, and I am doing it to the best of my ability. My duty is something I am designed to perform. Performance of duty should give a feeling of satisfaction – then what was the cause of this unjust state of mind? After further observation, I realised that people in all walks of life were getting burnt out by merely performing their duties and often dreamt of opting out, one day.

New beginnings gave rise to new curiosities in my mind. What is the definition of Duty? If performing one's Duty is the reason of one's existence then why do we see so many people getting frustrated and burnt out by merely performing their Duty? Is it the lack of understanding of one's Duty? Is it that the style of disbursement of Duty is questionable?

It's All In Our Hands

The general phenomenon of people getting frustrated and burnt out by merely fulfilling their basic duties as a bread-earner, home maker or a student made me ponder. Performance of our duty cannot be designed to have such negative effects. If performance of duty is part of one's existence, then the act should give satisfaction and happiness.

My father and myself were having a leisurely conversation during which he narrated an anecdote. He said, "Once there was a wise man who had a number of pupil in his hermitage. He prepared his pupils to step out in the real world and hence followed a strict routine. The wise man remained calm and composed and often seemed to be a boring old man. The students were a young and enthusiastic lot."

"On the day a batch of students were supposed to leave the hermitage, a congregation was called. The master was much revered among the pupil and there was a general consensus that his wisdom was beyond challenge. With all due respect to their master, the graduating students thought of a plan to achieve the unachievable, thus leaving a mark to remember them by. They thought of a plan to prove their master wrong by asking him a tricky question. When the master had finished his final address a departing pupil stood up with permission. After showering words of reverence, he held up his cupped hands and asked his master as to what was in his hands. 'A bird' replied the wise man. 'Dead or alive? asked the pupil. The pupil had planned that if the master's answer will be 'alive' the student will squeeze the bird to death and if his answer will be 'dead' the student will let the bird fly off.

"Foreseeing the plan to work, the students were excited to achieve the unachievable. They anticipated themselves as a batch that would be remembered for their clever trick – challenging the wisdom of the wisest man and getting one answer wrong from their revered master."

"The master thought for a while and finally replied, "It's all in your hands."

Yes. 'It's all in our hands'.

If performance of duty is part of existence, then it should give satisfaction and happiness.

CHAPTER THREE

GITA - THE KEY TO HAPPY LIVING

With the belief - it's all in our hands, I started my journey of seeking answers - Bhagavad Gita being the obvious beginning with its endless depth. Reading of the Bhagawad Gita gave me an understanding of duty. Duty is the responsibility of a person by virtue of birth and by virtue of the society he lives in.

Indian scriptures can be broadly divided into two categories:

a) Spirituality or the intangible existence, which includes topics like life after death or the existence of soul and the ultimate power (God).

b) The cosmic world or the tangible world that we live in.

These scriptures also acknowledged what I'd just realised after having spent half of my life – that feeling of suffering and frustration are bound to be felt even if we do not do anything wrong and are merely performing our duties. This acknowledgement had led to hundreds of years of work by many living souls. The wisdom thus compiled was put through practical usage evolving further over many lifetimes.

After much experience, our scriptures relating to the cosmic world have been compiled for the sole purpose of suggesting how to live a life in a state of happiness and discharge one's duty in an outstanding manner.

So my research on how to live a better quality of life and delivering above average performance towards one's duties began. I decided to spend few hours with my books and my thoughts over the weekends. This 'alone' time resulted in my wife, Neha, being inquisitive as to what I was up to. Just when I was looking forward to a happy Sunday with my books and thoughts she shot a funny but serious query. She did not mince words and startled me. She asked, "Are you planning to go to the mountains to become a renunciant or *sadhu*?"

I thought she was joking and like a true Indian MCP (male chauvinist pig) replied, "Don't be silly!"

As I sat on the dining table with the rest of the family I could sense some peering stares from my parents. But they held their arrows in the quiver till the kids left the table. As the last kid in the house vacated the dining room my dad asked in an authoritative voice, "What is your plan for the day?" This question reminded me of our summer vacations in school – it was a usual breakfast table question from him and we would always be ready with dribbling answers. But after so many years, I was not really anticipating this question. In a joint family, especially after marriage, we were never asked about our plans; more often than not as a practice we were supposed to inform everybody about our plans.

My mom asked me as to what I did for hours and where will it lead to. I explained my thoughts to them and reassured them that "I knew my duties and held them primary. I had observed among my friends as well as experienced myself that although we were doing very well in our corporate lives, we were not very happy. As I am inquisitive by nature, I'm digging into various sources of wisdom in books as to how we can be outstanding in performance of our duties and lead a happy and fulfilling life at the same time." This seemed to reassure them for now and thankfully, the conversation moved on to more lighter, comforting topics.

I'd chosen a comfortable corner in the house with minimum intrusion to do my answer-seeking. The Bhagavad Gita had various commentaries on it. In all there are only 700 verses in the Gita. What one interprets between the lines in the Gita is much more than what is originally written in it.

In my opinion, the mind of the writer of the commentary has to match the mindset of the reader to appeal to him. I'd read many commentaries; some propagated bhakti and complete surrender to Lord Krishna while others were more informative. Finally, what caught my interest was a commentary that dealt with the psychological aspects of the Bhagavad Gita.

After spending numerous weekends alone in my cozy corner, I decided to discuss with Neha as to where I could find good company to debate my findings. "Neha, I'm sure there are more people like me who are delving into the science of happy living," I consulted her one morning, immediately clarifying with a smile, "I mean non-renunciants."

As expected, first came the arrow before a thoughtful response, "Are you seeking a relationship outside?!" After spending more than a year filled with weekends in seclusion, digging into words of wisdom, she could justifiably accuse me of desertion, but this one was way out.

I politely replied, "Neha, I am not a stranger. You've known me for more than a decade. First you accuse me of running away from my responsibilities and now a new accusation?" As I said this, I suddenly realised, maybe I was not communicating enough with my wife. So we spent the rest of the day after lunch at a café. It was a fun day.

I realised that I was taking baby steps in the pursuit for answers but they were at least in the right direction. My career was moving towards growth, I was more disciplined and composed at work, and today I'd discovered a new kind of connect with my wife and in her I found a sensible and unconditional support structure. My wife, Neha, is a yoga instructor – an extremely well informed and well-read yoga practitioner. She's completed a course in Yoga sciences from the National Institute of Yoga and and thereafter her Msc in Yoga. She now runs her own yoga studio.

Our discussion that day had launched a series of post-dinner café visits. I'd found a like-minded companion to debate and discuss my research and findings and she'd been within my arms reach – all I'd had to do was open my eyes and look in the right direction.

Getting back to the conversation of me wanting to meet like-minded people, Neha and I pondered over visiting temples, mosques, churches, *madrasas*, etc. Finally, Neha came up with the suggestion of visiting libraries as a source of wisdom both in terms of books and interesting conversations.

The next weekend, I visited the British library and the American library. I informed the librarian of my field of interest, and they politely told me that such books were not available in their library. Then, I visited the Delhi Public Library and finally reached the Sahitya Kala Academy. As I was informing the librarian of my field of interest she interrupted me and introduced me to Mr. Vij. She told me that he was the guide I was looking for.

Mr. Vij guided me through the exhaustive collection of books in the library. The library holds more than two lakh books and is a priceless treasure for any seeker. It has scriptures of all the sects and in multiple languages. The reading room was serene and held the sanctity it deserved. I informed him of my quest and he welcomed me into this wonderful world. My discovery of like minded people in the library was a proof of an old saying 'You are what you read'.

Soon I became a regular to the library on weekends and my reading in solitude shifted to early mornings. I cut down on my jog time and started going to the park merely to breathe in some fresh air and indulge in a short jog of 10 minutes. After this, I spent an hour daily with my books and my thoughts. I started leading a more disciplined lifestyle and realised that a day well begun gave enough time to have all kinds of experiences one wants to seek. Twenty-four hours were enough to lead a healthy, thoughtful and dutiful life. An hour every day of thought-provoking reading changed my life. My productivity at work was improving, which was validated both by my brother and the results of the company.

I was, by now, a regular to the library. Over time, I got introduced to priceless scriptures like *Bhajgovindam*, *Atma*

Bodhah and *Tattvabodhah* of Adi Shankracharya, Nyaya Darshan and charvaka philosophies, Patanjali Sutras and also wisdom across other cultures with my reading of books like The Quran, The Bible, Guru Granth Sahib and books on Buddhism, Jainism. My understanding of man, his duty and the key to happy living was gaining form and definition.

You are what you read.

CHAPTER FOUR

TRIGUNAS - A SUCCESS MANTRA

One day, as I was digging deep into the shelves of the library looking for some works of Adi Shankracharya I came across a bunch of papers. The bunch was handwritten in ink that had blotted due to humidity. It was clearly evident that the papers had weathered over many seasons. The manuscript was written in Urdu. I had a little exposure to Urdu as my ancestral village was in the Urdu speaking part of undivided India. What caught my interest was the topic: "*Trigunas – My success Mantra*". The first page gave a small introduction about the writer.

Trigunas had always interested me. Chapter 14 in the commentry of Gita is entirely dedicated to *Trigunas*. Shri Krishna had given the knowledge of *Trigunas* to Arjuna as the formula to evolve successful in the battlefield. Merely stating the attributes of evolved living seems to be a fairytale. Evolved living as I understood was living with clarity of thought, discharging one's duty to the best of one's ability, and living a life without the delusions of emotions. The evolved mind is not disturbed by the extremes of excitement, sadness, anger, anxiety, nor is it distracted by the pursuit of pleasure.

However, it is easier said than done. The key to reach this detached and happy state of existence is the knowledge of the *Trigunas*.

From whatever little I could gather about the anonymous writer it was clear that he had taken a role of mentor in the latter part of his life. His writing and choice of language clearly indicated that he would be over 75 years as of date. His intention was to pass on his legacy of thoughts to the team in the company that he had built over years. This philosophy was what he attributed his success to. The meticulous write up was supposed to be his parting gift to his team and was to be printed in his company's quarterly magazine.

Shri Krishna gave the key to success to Arjuna in his times of despondence. When Arjuna was moments away from fighting the humongous army of the *Kauravas* in the battlefield, the fear of losing gripped his mind, not undermining his reverence of his own kith and kin. This is when Shri Krishna gives Arjuna the knowledge of the *Trigunas* to compete and emerge successful in the battle. Similarly, it seems that Mr. Anonymous wanted to share his success mantra of *Trigunas* before leaving the competitive corporate world. He wanted this mantra to drive his company to scale new heights just as he had led it to its present state.

My knowledge of Urdu is negligible and so I took the bunch of papers home – my father could translate it for me. I took out the first and the last page so as to hand over the main content to my father to translate. To avoid uncomfortable questions from my dad regarding Mr. Anonymous, I gave him the mantra and avoided the personal information pages.

My dad was delighted to see the Urdu manuscript. He was introduced to Urdu in school before the partition of India. Over the years he maintained his fondness of the language due to his interest in Urdu *ghazals*. His bedside books always had one of Ghalibs or Kahlil's poetry. He got down to translating without any queries.

Over the coming weekend I got a lot of questions from him regarding the origin and the mention of *Trigunas* in our scriptures. I could satisfy his curiosity because of the knowledge I had acquired over many weekends in the library and years of cozy corner reading at home.

One day, over morning tea, he said, "I am able to relate the *Gunas* to various personalities and their driving styles on the road."

I exclaimed, "That's a new one! Relation between driving styles on the road and *Gunas* will help me simplify an otherwise very serious subject."

Anxiously, I insisted on reading a few pages that he had translated. My curiosity on the subject was growing and finally he did give me part of his translation. I photocopied his translation and handed it over to my wife Neha too. It was just a few pages but our anxiety could not wait. Neha and I felt as if we were handed over the magic potion. After an early dinner we went to the café and started with our bunch of translated papers.

Shri Krishna gives Arjun the knowledge of Trigunas to compete and emerge successful in the battlefield.

CHAPTER FIVE

THE URDU MANUSCRIPT

Translated Text from the Manuscript:

Every human is made up of three *Gunas* namely, *Tamas*, *Rajas* and *Sattva*. All the three are omnipresent and determine the nature of a person. One of them is always dominating over the other two. Our behaviour, state of mind and nature of action is all determined by the *Gunas*. Our reaction in various circumstances is also determined by the *Gunas*.

The Bhagavad Gita has two chapters dedicated to *Trigunas*. Chapter 14 is the introduction and then later, Chapter 17 talks about nurturing the *Gunas*. Shri Krishna introduces *Trigunas* to Arjuna and also imparts the knowledge of how to cultivate and nurture them. The theory of *Trigunas* has also been mentioned in the *Upanishads*, which pre-date even the Gita and are a part of the Vedas, the existence of which dates back to 3000 BC. That means the theory of *Trigunas* has lived the test of time and therefore is worth the attention of every living soul.

Tamas is associated with the ultimate source – the basic five gross elements, i.e. earth, water, fire, air and ether. *Tamas* is a state of stillness. When manifested in a state of mind, it is associated with inaction, inertia, lethargy, sloth and confusion.

Rajas is associated with active organs i.e. hands, feet, mouth, eyes, organs of excretion and the reproductive organs. *Rajas* is a state of action. When manifested in a state of mind, it is associated with passion, aggression, initiative and emotions of anxiety, excitement or depression.

Sattva is associated with the cognitive senses, i.e. touch, taste, sound, smell and sight. *Sattva* is the state of pure intelligence. *Sattva* when manifested in a state of mind is associated with calmness, composure, contentment and equanimity.

Rajas is associated to creation, *Sattva* to preservation and *Tamas* to destruction. *Rajas* to red (vibrant), *Sattva* to white (subtle) and *Tamas* to black (darkness). And while *Rajas* is associated with the active organs, *Sattva* with sensations and *Tamas* is the medium or sense faculties without which no sensation can reach the sense organs, i.e. hearing or smelling is not possible without air, they all coexist.

A varying proportion of these three *Gunas* is what we see as the dynamic nature of a person. His behaviour and tendencies are an outcome of his *Gunas*. One of the three is always dominant over the other two but at the same time all three are always present in every human or as a matter of fact in everything.

The predominance of *Gunas* may change many times over a lifetime. When the *Sattva* is predominant and the *Rajas-Tamas* are dormant, one experiences composure, serenity and calmness. When the *Rajas* is predominant and *Sattva-Tamas* are dormant, one is active in the constant pursuit of pleasurable moments. Excessive

Rajas causes restlessness. The predominance of *Tamas* over *Rajas-Sattva* causes sleepiness, lethargy and inactive days. At any given time all the three *Gunas* are present, only the proportion varies.

Gunas determine the reaction of a personality to the circumstances he is exposed to. A composed reaction is a trait of *Sattva*, display of emotion is a trait of *Rajas* and the absence of reaction is a trait of *Tamas* dominance in a personality. Ironically, the absence of reaction of *Tamas* may seem externally similar to the composed reaction of the *Sattva* but the result of a composed reaction will lead to improvements whereas a result of absence of reaction will lead to stagnation.

Rajas is the only *Guna* capable of action, the other two are a state of being. A change in the proportion of *Gunas* can be instigated only by *Rajas* because change requires action. *Rajas* is the one that helps manifest the cause of a *Guna* to its effect.

All three *Gunas* have an importance in ideal existence in a human being. Without *Rajas*, no cause will manifest into an effect because any change needs activity. Without *Tamas*, there will be no stability in existence or consistency over a period of time.

The three *Gunas* can be cultivated and nurtured in oneself. The change in proportion of the Gunas manifests into a state of mind and affects the kind of day one has i.e. a peaceful day, an action packed day or a lethargic day. The *Gunas* can be cultivated by internal discipline and external discipline. Internal disciplines are methods that can be applied within ourselves and external disciplines are methods that we need to apply by choosing the circumstances we want to expose ourselves to. By conscious nurturing one can remain under the effect of a particular *Guna* over years, extended to a lifetime.

As we read through the concept page, the café staff started switching off the lights and indicated us to leave. Hot coffee, had turned cold by now. We looked into each other's eyes curious to know what the other felt about the concept, gulped our coffee in silence and sat in the car. After reading the concept pages I could relate more to what Dad was saying about the reflection of the *Gunas* in driving style.

The first paragraph itself was relevant: *Our behaviour, state of mind and nature of action are all determined by the Gunas. Our reaction to various circumstances is also determined by the Gunas.* Honking or sudden changing of lanes does reflect the *Rajas* trait of the driver. But at the same time, honking or changing of lanes may also be a requirement of the situation. So 'consciously' invoking *Rajas* may be indicative of an evolved state of mind. Mr. Anonymous has already stated, *All the three are omnipresent.* When the domination of *Rajas* is excessive and honking or lane changing becomes a way of driving, it can have dangerous repercussions for the driver.

Breaking the thoughtful silence, Neha questioned, "What do you mean that the *Trigunas* have survived the test of time?" Since my father was from the pharmaceutical industry I could relate this question to one of the products he had got formulated - a mix of Honey, Tulsi and Banaphsa. The product grew to be a big success. I introduced Neha to the concept of 'History of Safe Use' and replied, "History of Safe Use' is a term used in the pharmaceutical industry to say that this drug or concept need not be proven in the laboratory, as it has been used over a thousand years (eternally) and has proved its history of safe use. Similarly time has reinforced the concept of Trigunas."

The concept of *Trigunas* is mentioned in *Samkhya* philosophy and *Mandukya Upanishad*. Both these texts date back to 3000 BC and are one of the oldest texts available to mankind; they are part of the Vedas. The concept has sustained all eliminations and has again found mention in Gita of Mahabharata, dating back to 2000 BC. In *Patanjali Sutras* this concept of *Triguna* is mentioned again, i.e. approximately 500-200 BC. The stage before enlightenment, in Buddhism, is known as Bodhi*Sattva*, which is derived from the '*Sattva*' *Guna*. Buddhism came into existence around 500 BC and was rekindled by a Japanese scholar in the 13th Century AD. Innumerable philosophies thereon have reiterated the concept of *Trigunas*, including the philosophies written by Adi Shankracharya*ji* in 100 AD, gradually emerging to be a concept that cannot be neglected and can be safely classified as a 'History of Safe Use' since its origin and application dates back to over 4000 years.

Neha recalled reading a book to our daughter and said, "Hey, I remember a book: *Strange Case of Dr. Jekyll and Mr. Hyde*. This book is about split personality, much like the omnipresence of *Trigunas*."

I could relate a few Indian cricket personalities in terms of their reactions on field. MS Dhoni and Sachin Tendulkar always seemed so calm and composed even during extreme testing times. Neha spoke about the aggression and passion displayed by Sourav Ganguly and S Sreesanth. Ganguly taking off his T-Shirt in a state of excitement or Sreesanth murmuring abuses on field in a state of frustration seemed to reflect *Rajasik* reactions to testing circumstances. At the same time, *Rajasik* reactions of Ganguly were always well within the limits of 'positive sportsman spirit' but the abusive and aggressive stares of Sreesanth seemed to have a hint of 'negative sportsman spirit'. This may be due to the variation of *Tamas* in the two personalities, I concluded.

"It will be interesting to know the internal and external discipline to nurture the *Gunas*," Neha said. "Request Papa to give us those pages first."

I was quick to boast my newfound wisdom and remarked, "Don't display the anxiety of *Rajas*."

She smiled and we mutually decided to read the concept of *Gunas* again for better understanding. We knew this concept would be the basis of the entire bunch being translated. So we went back home and slept. Early in the morning, by 6 am, we went to our cozy corner and got deeply involved in rereading the *Triguna Mantra*.

Theory of Trigunas have stood the test of time. It is not a need but an opportunity.

CHAPTER SIX

TRIGUNAS – THE CONCEPT

Translation Continued

Bhagvad Gita helps us differentiate between 'Duty' and 'Attachment to the fruits of Duty'. Duty and the Attachment to its fruit are two different aspects. The *Gunas* of a person play an important role in our behaviour pattern.

Duty is the responsibility of a person by virtue of birth and by virtue of the society he lives in. By virtue of birth a person has duty towards his parents, brother, sister, other relatives and also towards *Prakriti* or Nature. Duty by virtue of society is duty towards his wife, children, his nation and as a householder also towards his occupation, to economically support his wife, children, the elders and the poor. Duty by virtue of being a wife will be as a homemaker. As a wife, she has a duty to nurture her children into good human beings and also take care of other family members.

In today's world the duty towards one's occupation is consuming substantial time and energy of a person. This excessive devotion of time and energy towards one's occupation is by choice because the fruits of duty towards occupation are easily measurable by wealth earned, whereas the fruits of Duty towards parents and kin are not easily measurable. They are long-term and

Trigunas – The Concept

bear fruits in terms of *karma* that carves out one's future circumstances. *Karma* is nothing but cause and effect.

So it is the Attachment to fruits of duty that is determining the importance of duty in one's life today and not the Duty itself. Elaborated ahead is how the nature of a person determines whether he is attached to the fruits of duty or whether he is dedicated to the duty itself.

Shri Krishna in Bhagwad Gita stresses on the importance of Duty itself and not on the fruits of Duty. As mentioned earlier, the nature of a person can be attributed to the *Gunas* present in him. So the graph ahead illustrates how the dominance of each *Guna* carves out the nature of a person. Further, how the nature of a person reflects in the dedication towards Duty and/or Attachment to fruits of duty. Before we proceed, it is important to take some time to reflect and understand the difference between dedication towards Duty and Attachment towards the fruits (outcome of action) of duty.

Mr. Anonymous had elaborated on the concept by representing the *Gunas* in a simple graph. We took his advice and assimilated our thoughts. Neha's eyes seemed to be overflowing with wisdom; she expressed her mind in a series of sentences: "This really simplifies our existence and removes our self-introduced complexities in life! We can actually list down our duties by virtue of birth and our stature in society."

Awaiting the interesting prioritisation, I sat in silence and she continued after a thoughtful moment. "Duty by virtue of my birth will be towards my parents, the health of my body, Duty of being conscious of the self-sustaining nature around us and not to cause undue damage to it." Hoping to hear my reference I sat in patience as she continued, "Duty by virtue of stature in society will include duty as a sister towards my brother, Duty to keep up the morals of the society and not to be a nuisance in it." I was still awaiting my reference as she continued to express her basic duties, "As I got married my Duty towards you and the family, raising of our kids into good human beings." And then came a mindful one, "As we gain knowledge by education and experience it also becomes our duty to discharge our priorities skillfully to the best of our abilities!"

She exclaimed, "With the awareness of one's duties, it suddenly feels so easy to focus on them and remove the delusions that we spend so much time on."

I was impressed and uttered, "Wow! This translation is really going to be a life maker." But I was intrigued and queried, "Neha, you defined Duty. How will you define Attachment towards fruits of duty?"

She answered, "These are my duties, awareness of my duties should lead to discharging them to the best of my ability. My attachment should be limited to discharging my duties to the best of my ability. The moment I start discharging my duty with lure towards its return, my attachment will not be towards the execution of duty but towards the fruits of discharging my duty."

"Insightful," I remarked. "I think this clarity of concept will help us understand the graphical representation of *Gunas*, their relationship with the Attachment towards Duty and Attachment towards the fruits of performing our Duty."

We got back to the last of translation that we had received from dad for the time being.

Duty is the responsibility of a person by virtue of birth and by virtue of the society he lives in.

CHAPTER SEVEN

DUTY AND ATTACHMENT

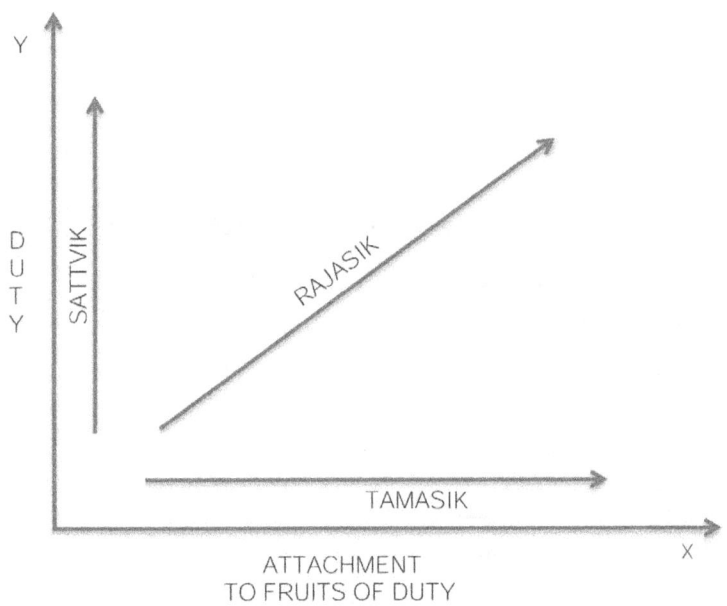

As we can see, a person with dominating *Tamas Guna* has an everlasting increase in desire (Attachment to fruits of Duty) whereas his will or dedication towards doing his duty does not increase. He is lethargic and the will to perform his duty is therefore missing. This person is high on desire (attachment) towards the fruits of duty (money, fame, love, and materialistic possessions) but low on the will to perform duty. With dominance of the *Tamas Guna* comes dullness and stagnancy in life. Desires of a person may even push him to fulfilling them by indulging in anti-social activities.

A *Rajasik* person is action-oriented. His sense of duty and attachment to the fruits of duty grow hand in hand. He is focused on the fruits and also performs his duty with zeal and enthusiasm. He works for incentives. Such people are successful when measured in wealth accumulation. The only drawback being, they remain tensed, as they are worried about the outcome of their actions.

They are prone to extreme excitement and depression as they take success and failure to heart. All actions cannot lead to success, therefore every failure drains them and there is a chance of hitting a break point in life. They measure their success with fruits of their action, namely wealth and fame. The only issue is the desire for more everlasting wealth and fame. This desire is his driving force but leaves him ever discontented. Setbacks lead to frustration that leads to losing focus and getting confused.

Setbacks make them contemplate in confusion as to what their purpose of life is. This Lifestyle is known as *Kamya Karma*. Working to fulfill desires. Excessive *Rajas* supported by *Tamas* can lead to serious anti-social activities. To fulfill excessive desires, a person may take to theft, rape or fraud.

Intense *Rajas* supported by *Sattva* may make a person very wealthy but highly tensed. This wealthy and stressed person is prone to reach a limit of frustration and run away from his duties to solitude. The sacred path of renunciation followed after frustrations in *Kamya Karma* is a path of dishonour. One merely becomes a burden on the society.

A *Sattvik* person has a high sense of duty. As you can see in the graph, he is completely focused on his duty and not on the fruits of duty. He is calm and composed. That does not mean he is under-performing in any way. He is a calm and composed person, working to the best of his abilities. The tension of fruits or outcome do not bother him but are a measure of the performance of duty and facilitates improvement. He is unstoppable by failure. He has his eye on the outcome but that is to improve or review his performance and not to feed his ego. His sense of duty is ever growing and does not decline with setbacks. This kind of lifestyle is known as *Nishkam Karma* or *Kartavya Karma*. Work done with focus on one's duty or *Kartavya*.

There is a difference between good and pleasure. Everything that is pleasurable need not be good and vice versa. A pleasant action is meant to pleasure the senses of a human being and good action is for the overall goodness. *Rajas* is important for manifesting a state of mind to act and achieve results, but excess of *Rajas* leads to pleasure seeking which is not good. Therefore, a dominating *Sattva* supported by *Rajas* and thus minimising *Tamas* is a good combination to nurture.

The Dominance of *Sattva* is delightful and also helps to maintain a mental and emotional balance. A person with a weak *Sattva Guna* may develop mental or emotional disorders. An excess of *Rajas* supported by *Tamas* and a weak *Sattva* can lead to an undesired personality in the society. If you ask a shoplifter, he will acknowledge his wrong action. A person with excess *Rajas* and a very weak *Sattva* gets involved in ill actions unconsciously and has no idea what made him do so.

Duty And Attachment

Every human being is born with all three *Gunas*. A person can nurture one *Guna* and make it dominant over the other two. Nurturing a *Guna* can be done by internal discipline and external discipline as mentioned earlier.

If you study legendary personalities, I mean legendary and not merely above average, you will observe traits matching with those pertaining to dominance of *Sattva*. The outcome of their duty does not show in their expression or in all probability it does not even disturb them too much. Outcome is definitely a measure of their performance and impacts improvement strategy. Plotting this kind of a nature in the graph will prove dominance of *Sattva Guna* in their nature.

The dominance of any one of the *Gunas* results in certain outwardly symptoms. For example, a *Rajasik* person likes steaming hot tea, spicy food and tends to eat fast. Whereas a *Sattvik* person will like food with fewer spices and will take more time finishing his meal. A *Rajasik* dominant person displays passion, excitement, sadness or anger. A *Sattvik* dominant person will display calmness, warmth, composure and contentment. A *Tamasik* person will also seem calm from the outside but that will be due to his inactive and lethargic state of mind.

A *Rajasik* dominant person will carry a lot of flaunt-worthy items and will like to talk about his wealth (fruits of action) as he is attached to the same. A *Rajasik* person will be able to impress people in the first meet itself. On the contrary, a *Sattvik* person may seem boring in the first meeting. The same can also be said about a *Tamasik* dominant person; he might also seem boring in the first meeting.

A *Tamasik* person can evidently look calm and composed whereas he may be in a state of sleepiness and inaction. An aspirant should not allow *Tamasik* qualities to grow in his head. He should prevent his mind from going into the grooves of negativity and passivity. A *Rajasik* dominant, successful person when exposed to excessive stress and temporary failure, can very easily slip back into a *Tamasik* phase.

Gunas have a gradual progression, which cannot be skipped. It is important to give *Rajasik* incentives to a *Tamasik* person to spring into action and only then can he progress to *Sattvik* traits. Non-*karma* (inertia) can be shattered by *Kamya Karma* (work for desire fulfillment) and be further evolved to a state of *Kartavya Karma*.

An average person's lifetime may see the dominance of various *Gunas* in various phases of life. The dominance of one *Guna* may or may not be consistent all through life. A *Guna* can be inculcated by suitable habits. A *Guna* can be fed and nurtured to dominate the other two *Gunas*. The scriptures also prescribe habits and dietary plans to nurture a particular *Guna*.

As we finished reading the translation of this part, our respect for Mr. Anonymous scaled new heights. His clarity of thought was certainly commendable.

Neha was quick to get back to cricket personalities. "Mahendra Singh Dhoni has a similar lack of expression on field. He has led India to be the number one team in the world. A similar calmness and composure is also evident in Sachin Tendulkar. Both personalities can be termed legendary and also display attributes of *Sattvik* dominance."

The discussion over personalities evolved to identify different combinations of *Gunas* and its outwardly effects.

Sreesanth, the famous cricketer was always known to be very expressive on field. He was a young, promising pace bowler who was named the 'Man of The Match' for his outstanding performance in South Africa in 2006. He had taken 5 wickets, giving away only 40 runs.

On the field, he would get excited and dance over taking a wicket. Or get depressed with teary eyes over losing a match. It was this *Rajasik* dominance that had catapulted him to becoming a very successful cricketer. He gained excellence and reached commendable heights in the world of cricket at a very young age. But it can probably be said that soon his *Rajas* grew beyond appreciable levels. In two simultaneous incidents his conduct was seen as a display of negative spirit in the game and he was penalised up to fifty percent of the match fees. His aggressive stares progressed on to running after the batsman after taking his wicket, as he did with Hashim Amla, to physically shouldering the English captain, Michel Vaughan.

With reference to the news regarding his alleged involvement in match fixing we further analysed his phases in life and concluded, "It seemed that in his nature the *Rajas* got nurtured beyond optimum levels. His desire for objects of pleasure grew beyond his capacity. Although he was earning more than 20 million a year with Indian Premier League (IPL) matches and other endorsements, his desires were ever-growing. When the authorities were accounting for the cash that he allegedly earned by deceiving means, it was reported in the *Times of India* that he had spent more than two lakhs on designer clothes, including a pair of high-end jeans. A senior police officer was quoted saying, "He made cash payments and even spent lavishly in clubs and discotheques."

"Two lakhs for jeans and clothes shopping in a single day was a need he fulfilled." I concluded. "Such can be the effects of nurturing the wrong combination of *Gunas*."

Despite the clean chit given by the lower courts, the BCCI had decided to continue the ban on him as of now.

Our discussion further gave clarity to the concept of *Gunas*. We felt enriched with our newfound wisdom. Rearing to do our duties in life with a better approach we parted with silent enthusiasm. Somewhere inside, both of us wanted to meet our new friend, Mr. Anonymous.

While I was driving to office the next day, I visualised Mr. Anonymous to be a calm and composed person with aggressiveness at will. Building an organisation of a level that takes out quarterly magazines for its employees meant the organisation must have an employee count of over a thousand. The organisation could be spread across geographies. He must be a first generation entrepreneur who had faced enough struggles to gain such wisdom. His write-up seemed more experiential than theoretical. "It will certainly be a pleasure and a learning experience to meet him some day," I thought to myself.

The day at office had its usual set of crises management. After lunch we generally have a little free time and get involved in more productive work like evaluating Key Result Areas of team members. As mentioned earlier, our company was growing at a good pace and I had a meeting with the sale team in the evening. The whole purpose of the meeting was to announce a new incentive scheme for the month to get them motivated for achieving their targets.

Duty And Attachment

I suddenly remembered reading the word incentive this morning in the *Triguna Mantra* of Mr. Anonymous. I realised that incentive is nothing but the 'fruit of action'. I realised that motivating them to earn their incentive is actually trying to increase their attachment to the 'Fruits of Duty' rather than Duty itself. Now this was contradictory to my newly-found wisdom. I decided to go ahead as usual with my meeting with the sales team and get back to the *Triguna Mantra* after dinner to get clarity.

Over dinner, Neha requested Dad to expedite the translation. After dinner we drove to the café. On the way I told Neha about my confusion. We decided to read the relevant part together.

'A Rajas person is action oriented. His sense of duty and attachment to the fruits of duty grow hand in hand. He is focused on the fruits and does his duty with zeal and enthusiasm. He works for incentives. Such people are successful when measured in wealth accumulation. The only drawback being, they remain tense as they are worried about the outcome of their actions'.

Immediately after we finished reading, I acknowledged, "Neha, come to think of it this is exactly what we want from our team," I continued, holding the translated bunch in my hand. "In the corporate world we want people to do their duty with zeal and enthusiasm. He works for incentives. Such people are successful when measured in wealth accumulation." I completed my sentence by reading out of the Mantra paper.

"For the stress and tension, the offshoots of *Rajas*, the corporate world has created a separate department of Human

Resources who is supposed deal with it. There is a separate budget sanctioned for employees to involve them in stress buster activities periodically. All this sounds quite organised now!" I exclaimed. "So in the corporate world, all processes are designed to nurture *Rajas* for immediate results, that is why companies are talking about stress management all the time because stress is an obvious offshoot of *Rajas*," I concluded.

"But then Mr. Anonymous has clearly stated that dominating *Sattva* supported by *Rajas* and thus minimising *Tamas* is a good combination," queried Neha.

I was quick to read through the bunch, *"If you study legendary personalities, I mean legendary and not merely above average, you will observe traits matching with those pertaining to the dominance of Sattva."* Neha, most of the middle-level motivational or training programmes are designed to get above average performance and not legendary performance," I continued. "Legends are self-motivated people, focused on their duty; they are not distracted by materialistic baits. They are people who continue to walk their path unweathered by a win or loss of a battle on the way. The loss in battles merely adds to their learning experiences. They are bound to win the war and attain legendary status. Such may be the outcome of *Sattva* dominance," I concluded.

While I was reading aloud from the bunch of papers, I realised another paragraph was relevant to the situation under the scanner. I continued reading aloud to Neha: *"Gunas have a gradual progression, which cannot be skipped. It is important to give Rajasik incentives to a Tamasik person to spring into action and only then can he progress to Sattvik traits. Non-karma (inertia) can be shattered by Kamya Karma (work for desire fulfillment) and only then be further evolved to a state of Kartavya Karma. When dealing with middle management in the meeting room to achieve a common goal we do not know the set of Guna traits in the group. Kamya Karma is the safest bet to achieve our group goal."*

"Today you seem to be quite clear in your thoughts," Neha remarked. I realised that experiences in work life certainly help connect a lot of dots. I understood that the key to evolving from average productivity to outstanding productivity lies in nurturing the right *Gunas*. That was the secret behind the outstanding performance of Mr. Anonymous. He seemed to have learnt and implemented this process of nurturing the right set of *Gunas* and after experiencing success he wanted to pass on the *Triguna Mantras* to his team members.

Days went by and we continued to discuss the concept. The concept of *Trigunas* could be related to any personality and helped us analyse various circumstances. We were curious to know the process of internal and external discipline to nurture the *Gunas*. That would also put light on the kind of lifestyle Mr. Anonymous was leading. Dad had confirmed that the papers on nurturing process could be expected soon. The date of my departing for the Maha Kumbh *Mela* was nearing too.

One day, Neha made an interesting reference and said, "Mother Teresa must be an example of pure *Sattva*." She continued, "A personality that is primarily known for her compassion, peace and love."

"Now that is interesting," I remarked.

What came next from Neha was insightful. "At the same time, we have to appreciate the action component in her as well. It is the *Rajasik* action component that led her *Sattva* attributes of compassion and love to conclusive results. So we can see a dominance of *Sattva* supported by *Rajas* that made her an outstanding personality."

Mother Teresa's example clearly stated that *Rajas* was the *Guna* of action. *Rajas* is the *Guna* that manifests the attributes of *Sattva* or *Tamas* in the real world. All these discussions and analysis made us realise that the ability to consciously nurture one's *Gunas* must be a blissful act.

Neha reiterated what we both were thinking, "Please request Dad to give us the translation on the nurturing of the *Gunas*."

My trip to the Kumbh *Mela* was a sour topic between us. It was sour because of an obvious reason: 'I was going there alone'. I tried to explain that I was intrigued by the fact that the Kumbh *Mela* was the largest spiritual congregation of people in the world. I was looking forward to meet some interesting people and discuss different philosophies of various sects, specially the *Naga Sadhus*. I hoped that I get to have meaningful conversations. And I now had the *Triguna Mantra* to discuss and receive new perspectives on the subject.

After my trips to the library since a year, I realised that meeting people from different walks of life and indulging in intricate discussions really gives new dimensions to a subject.

On the dinner table dad appreciated Mr. Anonymous's command over the Urdu Language and said "This man is most certainly older than me, his command over Urdu shows that he has studied in an Urdu medium school for very many years. Whether he is alive or not his philosophy is certainly guiding many living souls to success through this compilation."

Dad assured to give me the next set of papers over the coming weekend. We eagerly awaited to decipher the secret *Triguna Mantra*. Finally, on Saturday we got our translated source of wisdom. We immediately moved to our cozy corner and started to read.

For a Sattvik personality result is only a measure of performance to facilitate improvement, without any emotional attachment to it.

CHAPTER EIGHT

SEQUENTIAL PROGRESSION OF *TRIGUNAS*

As mentioned earlier, the evolvement of *Gunas* can only happen in gradual progression. That is, from *Tamas* to *Rajas* to *Sattva*. The evolvement from *Tamas* to *Rajas* is the only route to *Sattva*. Solution to break through *Tamas* is *Kamya Karma*. *Kamya Karma* is working for the want of material desires. Desire for a bigger car, house, expensive clothing, etc. *Kamya Karma* is certainly useful for shattering *Tamas*. After shattering the *Tamas* and evolving into *Rajas*, further nurturing can be done to evolve to *Sattva* i.e *Kartavya Karma*. *Kartavya Karma* is working with dedication and discipline for the want of performing one's duties and not for the material desires it may fulfil. So a person has to first become aware of the predominance of *Guna* in him at the present stage and then tread the path.

Tamas through sleep, lethargy and ignorance are all states of pleasure. These pleasurable, seemingly happy states have a great pull towards themselves. What one does not foresee in this pleasurable happy state of *Tamas* is that it is bound to be followed by an unhappy phase. A lethargic lazy person will not fulfil his duties and end up in trouble. He will not be able to fulfil his basic needs of food, shelter and safety, let alone his desires.

Rajas, on the other hand, is all about action; he is desirous of his much-anticipated effects (fruit of action). Under the cause and effect phenomenon, the action becomes the cause that lead him to his desirous effect. The effect in all probability may be positive if the effort is right. Temporary setbacks are part of any success story. These temporary setbacks do not seem temporary in those moments. A *Rajasik* person may not be able to see beyond a temporary setback and this may result in shattering of his courage to continue. Therefore, too much *Kamya Karma* may leave a person unsatisfied as desires are ever increasing. Excessive *Rajas* may lead to stress and frustrations. There is a break point, a limit till which one can take the stress and difficulties. After the break point one is prone to get pushed towards the lethargic *Tamas*. A substantial percentage of people live a lifetime under the *Rajas* phase and never even attempt to evolve.

Another important aspect to be noted is that the blissful ignorance of *Tamas* has an intense pull. This pull increases when the push towards *Tamas* comes into play because of stress and tensions of *Rajas*. As mentioned earlier, all three *Gunas* are omnipresent and coexist in every personality. The breaking point from *Rajas* to fall back into blissful, lazy *Tamas* may come either because of increase in the pull of lazy *Tamas* or increase in the push from stressful *Rajas*. Renunciation becomes a pretentious offshoot of such a fall from *Rajas* to *Tamas*. Renunciation because of stress and frustrations of *Rajas* is a common phenomenon. Such renunciants are people who could not balance their lives. They were too attached to be aware or open to the concept of detachment.

Taking a holiday is very prominent nowadays in the urban lifestyle. The increase in periodicity of holidays in urban living is because it acts as a stress buster of

Sequential Progression Of Trigunas

the otherwise *Rajasik* lifestyle. These frequent breaks become necessary in todays lifestyle where our *Aahaar* (eating habits), *Vihaar* (recreation) and *Achaar* (routine) are all more aligned to nurturing *Rajas*. We tend to blame our preoccupation or profession for this stress, which is certainly not true. Our preoccupation is part of our duty, it is the attachments and the lifestyle that cause this stress. Nurturing of *Sattva* increases productivity in professional life and also helps living a stress-free and happy life.

A very popular movie, *Rocky*, has a famous dialogue narrated by Rocky Balboa, a boxer who was also the hero of the movie: "It ain't about how hard you hit. It's about how hard you can get hit and keep moving forward; how much you can take and keep moving forward."

In action (*Rajas*) you are bound to face difficulties (punches). It is important to fight the pull of *Tamas*, to stand up again after being hit by difficulties. The push of *Rajas* towards *Tamas* will always remain because of difficulties on the path of action. It is only when one evolves to *Kartavya Karma* of *Sattva* that the path of action remains the same but the frustrations vanish. He is neither pulled down by a failure nor gets disillusioned in the excitement of success.

Bhagavad Gita has many narrations and interpretations. In the first chapter, when Arjuna is reluctant to fight the battle, Shri Krishna helps him remove his despondence by giving him the knowledge of Gita. The dictionary meaning of despondence is 'a state of low spirits caused by loss of hope or courage'. After seeing the humongous army of the Kauravas, Arjuna lost hope of winning the battle. Arjuna's mind got diverted towards the result of the battle and the reason why he was actually fighting got lost in his mind. He went into a state of disillusion because he lost the cause or the sense of duty and got engulfed by the fear of negative result. Not to negate his emotional reluctance to fight his own kin and guru, his state of despondence was because of his attachment to the result and not to his duty. His attachment to the result caused stress, fear, tension, disillusion and discouragement.

For a second, imagine the visual: Arjuna is minutes away from fighting the humongous army facing him in the battlefield of Kurukshetra. He is about to fight an army that has his own guru and many other decorated warriors. All his life he has revered the competency of the ones he is about to fight. He is cognizant of the fact that one of the armies will certainly perish. Imagine his state of mind. Our tensions and stress in the corporate scenario seem minuscule in front of his in the battlefield. Shri Krishna sensed this state of mind. The battle had to be fought as part of Arjuna's duty and for the good of the society.

At this point, Shri Krishna helped Arjuna realign his thoughts towards his duty and helped him detach his mind from the result. And so the most popular thought as preached by Gita is to focus on the duty and not think about the results. When Arjuna queried further into how this state of focus could be achieved, Shri Krishna reveals the knowledge of self, meditation and *Triguna*, among other subjects.

Renunciation and Service

A lifestyle of self-restraint and service to the underprivileged helps evolve oneself from *Kamya Karma* to *Kartavya Karma*. In the *Kamya Karma* phase, one tends to enjoy life by fulfilling one's desires (this lifestyle is mentioned in *Charvaka* Philosphy). As we know that desires are unending and keep increasing, there comes a point when one feels frustrated and stressed out. At this transforming point it is important to evolve into the next state of *Kartavya Karma* and not slip into a *Tamasik* lifestyle.

Renouncing under the dominance of *Rajas* or *Tamas* is renouncing under confusion, disappointment and frustration. One cannot tread the path of evolvement with these feelings but can only drown in the darkness of ignorance. Renouncing is a very evolved path of spirituality and only a *Sattvik* person is capable of treading this path to realise the highest human potential. If one renounces the world because of fear, pain or frustration, he gives a bad name to the revered path of renouncement. As mentioned, only a *Sattvik* person is capable of following the revered path in its true spirit.

Rajas or attachment brings with itself the superfluous pair of opposites. *Rajas* is known for its involvement in pleasurable activities. Pleasure should not be confused with goodness. Pleasurable activities are ones that give pleasure or satisfy the senses of an individual. All sensory perceptions create a pair of opposites: pain and pleasure, sorrow and joy, heat and cold. One opposite can only be defined using the other extreme and therefore, both opposites coexist. Under the dominance of *Rajas*, the senses are most active and so the opposites are most frequently experienced. If a person feels excited sooner or later he shall also feel depressed. It is when one becomes aware of this reality that he starts to progress towards *Sattva*. Under the influence of *Sattva* one detaches from this web of superfluous opposites. A *Sattvik* person is free from likes and dislikes, he frees himself from the emotional outbursts and does not get confused by these pairs of opposites. Thus, he attains clarity of mind.

A *Sattvik* person is prone to the path of renunciation and this is one of the perils that poses a danger in the society. This inclination of a *Sattvik* person to leave the society and live in solitude reduces the overall influence of *Sattva* in the society. In the absence of *Sattvik* people the *Tamas* tends to dominate the society. A Sattvik person may leave the society to practice his austerities and then come back to contribute to his society. He must realise that such renunciation is going to give him personal gain whereas the society might need his influence and work so as to keep the *Tamas* in control.

Since personalities can be evidently categorised as *Sattvik*, *Rajasik* or *Tamas*ik and all three are omnipresent in each personality, so is true for a society. All societies are always a mix of all three kinds of personalities and will continue to be so. Even if a *Sattvik* person feels inclined to go into solitude, leaving the society, he must do so to tread his path of evolvement and come back to the society to contribute *Sattvik* influence to it.

A society in which more people are *Sattvik* will exude compassion, love and serenity. There will always be people who cause disturbance and anti-social activities. A *Sattvik* person should be aware of his need in the society for the overall goodness. He should discharge his duties in the society, thus leading an exemplary life.

All three *Gunas* have their importance in a society. Without *Tamas* there will be no stability. *Tamas* gives the trait of inertia without which the society will become too dynamic for human comfort. *Tamas* is responsible for giving gross and stable forms to all the elements. *Rajas* is responsible for the change and action in the society and *Sattva* is the guiding light. Even an anti-social person in the society will have a wish to be a part of the *Sattvik* society. This is because of the overall predominance of *Sattva* in the society.

Service to others gives us the joy of giving. It helps us overcome our instinctive 'I, Me, My' style of thinking. Service to others helps us reduce our ego quotient. Of course, this charity or social work will have its effect only if it is not driven by name, fame or wealth motives. Otherwise, the essence of reducing one's ego by service to others is lost. Reducing one's ego helps self-control as one is not in the race of flaunting. Ego-gratification is one of the biggest reasons why one acquires materialistic possessions.

We were feeling unusually anxious about reading the nurturing process since we were sure we'll start adhering to it. We realised that like many other instincts it is also instinctive of a human being to want to be a better person. Although Neha and I did not feel like we had extraordinary shortcomings or were low on self-confidence, we were looking forward to improve. I added to this enriching conversation of instincts and said, "I remember having read this in one of the books that these philosophies or wisdom are not a need for living. Life, any way can be fun and satisfying. These philosophies clears the mind of delusions thus making it more focused to achieve excellence."

Neha queried, "Then why this 'want' to be a better person?"

I reiterated, "It's instinctive."

"So," she continued, "this philosophy of *Trigunas* is certainly not a need but an opportunity."

"Yes," I replied.

From Neha's expressions it seemed that she had found her answers in the conversation but wanted to continue it, to have more clarity of thought. "I have seen many a people enjoying life from pleasure to pleasure. Then why deprive one's self of it?" She went on to answer her query herself, "These philosophies are a source of wisdom. They come handy in rough patches of life. A lifetime can easily be spent from pleasure to pleasure provided luck is on your side and you don't face any rough patches, right?"

"These philosophies become a way of life. They are not tools that can be used at will, as it sounds. I have seen many examples of people spending their life from pleasure to pleasure and crashing on difficult patches." Coming back to the point I continued, "These philosophies are a way of life that can pull you through all kinds of phases and make you an outstanding performer in whatever you do. They are certainly not a need; a person is designed to lead a good satisfying life any which way, provided he does not go to extremes." I remembered what my father always said, "One who knows when to stop falls into no danger."

We started discussing personalities who have often been in the news for their good times and flaunting lifestyle. One of the names that came to mind was Mr. Vijay Mallya, the 'king of good times'. Mr. Mallya's excessive involvement in sense pleasures may have caused neglect in profession that led to his down fall. "Wisdom can come by accessing the source or more importantly, by experience. I am sure the experiences of Mr. Mallya must have made him wiser."

"Neha, I think we are becoming more and more judgemental about famous personalities like Dhoni, Tendulkar, and now Mr. Mallya. I don't feel we have the right to do so."

Neha opined, "We are only using them as examples to understand and analyse our concepts. I am sure you and I do not have any ill feelings for any of the personalities that we are talking about." She did seem to make sense. I freed myself of the guilt as it was a fact. Talking about these personalities as examples was helping us understand the concept of *Trigunas* better.

Dad gave us the much awaited part regarding nurturing of the *Gunas*. We wanted to peek in but waited for the chance to steal some undisturbed time. We wanted to read as much as possible before my trip. Neha was kind to acknowledge that reading the translation was more insightful together and she would wait to continue the sessions with me rather than read while I was away. These sessions were also a blessing to our relationship. I also owed this new connect with my wife to Mr. Anonymous.

Wisdom clears the mind of delusions thus making it more focused to achieve excellence.

CHAPTER NINE

TILLING & NURTURING

Tilling

The source of wisdom is known to all and I have seen people queueing for it. I have met a lot of people who have enjoyed the experience of the source, with or without any impact on self. Different people perceive different streams as their source. One thing is definite: 'each and every individual has an inherent wish to become a wiser person'.

There is a certain preparedness of mind that is required to maximise assimilation from the source of wisdom. This preparedness usually comes from experiencing different phases of life. There are some sources that have proven validity either in laboratories or by the test of time. When a mind is prepared, it experiences a pull from the source and the learning is inevitable, like a seed sown in land is bound to grow into a beautiful plant provided the land has been worked upon to make it fertile. Likewise, only a prepared mind can nurture the seed of wisdom sown in it.

Age has nothing to do with preparedness. One may be of young age with the maturity of an adult or one may be an adult but immature and childish. It is the experiences in life and what one assimilates from them that brings preparedness. The ability to contemplate is what brings long-lasting learning. The mind should be made into a sponge with a contemplative discriminating layer.

If the source is in the form of a book, it should not be read like a novel. If one continues to read beyond 20 percent of the book he can be categorised as an aspirant. A person should be receptive to knowledge. If he has the love for wisdom he may continue to read using his own discriminating power. If the knowledge aligns with his discriminating power, there is nothing that will stop him to align his life to the knowledge thus gained.

"Validation in laboratories and test of time is in alignment with your pharmaceutical concept of 'history of safe use'," Neha commented.

"Yeah," I responded. "Tilling of the mind seems to be an interesting start."

We continued reading.

Nurturing Gunas by Discipline

I have personally disciplined myself to nurture *Gunas* in a predetermined proportion. It has made my working and personal life much more peaceful, productive and happy. My reactions to actions are different and later I have analysed the change and thanked God for the awareness he blessed me with. I have constantly dug into the wisdom in our scriptures for decades. Our scriptures have been preserved for over 4000 years; many great souls have contributed to the wisdom written in the scriptures. The concept of *Gunas* has been repeatedly mentioned through the ages and has sustained existence despite many philosophies being eliminated. Personally, I guarantee better performance in whatever one does as his duty and also a blissful family life. Results are certainly the measure of one's performance and are important for reviews and future improvements. What I am propagating is to reduce personal attachment to the results.

A lot of energy is drained in emotions. Emotional phases can also distract the course of action and thereby losing focus. Attaching oneself to the anticipated results can generate enthusiastic pursuit. Enthusiasm is good for achieving goals. But over enthusiasm is the enemy of perseverance in the long term. Temporary setbacks in enthusiastic pursuits will restrain the mind to improvise and try again, rather, it will lead to fatigue and loss of focus. Performance of duty with dedication and discipline can give tremendous results in the long term.

Nurturing of a *Guna* has to be inculcated in one's lifestyle. It is not a phase or periodic activity. The lifestyle of a person is already nurturing *Gunas* in him, the only difference being that he is unaware of the nurturing process. Nurturing the right *Guna* improves results without letting frustration creep in. Whether one is a student, housewife or a working professional, frustration or tensions only limit one's performance and can never be an enhancer. A state of awareness is always better than a state of ignorance. The fact that you are even reading this for creating a state of awareness shows a substantial component of *Rajas* in your personality. And the fact that I am writing this means I also have a substantial component of *Rajas* in my personality.

There will be many slips from the predetermined course of nurturing or *sadhana* (perseverance). A slip in the initial phases is a blessing in disguise. The slip phase makes one aware of the kind of productivity one was churning out in the phase of discipline or *sadhana*. Sadhana is very personal and requires an initial effort.

After an aspirant experiences the life of *sadhana* over a period of a year he yearns to repeat the same. In the process of yearning to repeat the phase, the aspirant reaches new heights of *sadhana* and experiences life and productivity beyond aspirations.

After an initial phase of discipline which continued for approximately two years, I slipped; my discipline deteriorated. In the deteriorated phase I was awestruck when I retrospectively thought of my productivity at work and writing during the past two years. It was as if I was merely an instrument or a tool working effortlessly, personifying brilliance. It is important to come back from the slipped deteriorated phase and reinstate one's course of *sadhana*. The bouncing back requires awareness and some effort.

Rajas is a very powerful *Guna*. It is a *Guna* of action. A predominance of *Rajas* when supported with *Sattva* can lead to a successful phase. *Rajas* when supported with *Tamas* can lead to negative mindset leading to destruction, crime and unsocial activities.

Sattva, when supported with *Tamas* can also have ill-effects. For example, Bhishma Pitamaha, a revered character, was seen as wisdom personified and protector of the Hastinapur province in the scripture, *Mahabharata*. Undoubtedly, he had the predominance of *Sattva*. To describe his level of evolvement further, he had the boon to choose his time of death. At the same time, he was not a free man.

The element of freedom decreases from *Sattva* to *Rajas* to *Tamas*. His *Sattva* was supported by *Tamas*; he was chained by his own mindset and self-restraining vows. He had limited his own freedom by the *Tamasik* thoughts in him; his own vows took away his freedom to act. It was the *Tamas* in him that did not allow him to stop the molestation of a princess in front of his eyes. He exhibited inertia of the mind and could not uphold the morals of the society. The *Sattva* in him was supported by *Tamas* and he had a weak *Rajas* component.

However, predominance of *Sattva* supported by *Rajas* can catapult a person to above average performance and tremendous success.

Neha interrupted with an interesting comparison and said, "There seems to be a resemblance between Bhishma Pitamaha and Dr. Manmohan Singh, our ex-Prime Minister." I was a little amused by the comparison but it seemed interesting.

She elaborated, "Prime Minister Manmohan Singh was known for his silence and lack of expression. Lack of expression can be interpreted as lack of excitement (*Sattva*) or lack of action (*Tamas*). At the same time, one can acknowledge that his tenure as Finance Minister and later as Prime Minister during his first tenure saw impactful performance. Whether it was economic liberalisation or the nuclear deal or 8% GDP growth. He was undoubtedly known to be honest and non-corrupt. But during his second tenure he seemed to be chained, just like Bhishma Pitamaha; blatant corruption and scams happened and he did not take any action to prevent them. Given his reputation, it seems to be a similar inertia in the mind chained by vows of being a custodian of power."

It was definitely an interesting comparison. I added "The *Rajas* in both cases was so weak that the attributes of the dominant *Sattva* could not manifest themselves in the real world."

Case studies like these of different personalities were quite insightful. For instance, the *Sattva* in Mother Teresa was supported by *Rajas*, which possibly gave her the ability to manifest the attributes of love and compassion in the real world. Whereas the *Sattva* in Bhishma Pitamaha in *Mahabharata* was supported by *Tamas*, which plagued the righteousness of *Sattva* with the *Rajas* being too weak to convert attributes into action.

Neha also appreciated Mr. Anonymous and said, "Going by the confidence by which Mr. Anonymous guarantees performance, he seems to be a revered personality, who is sure his testimonial will be impactful in his organisation."

Taking the opportunity of the untimely break in reading I expressed my opinion, "It seems Mr. Anonymous is certainly a visionary. His organisation must have a very low attrition ratio; I mean employees must be sticking on in his company for longer periods of time than the usual scenario in the corporate world."

Neha was waiting for me to justify this opinion and I read out a few lines from the *Triguna Mantra*, "*Enthusiasm is good for achieving goals. But over enthusiasm is the enemy of perseverance in the long term. Temporary setbacks when involved in enthusiastic pursuit will restrain the mind to improvise and try again, or it may lead to fatigue and one will tend to loose focus.*"

"Generally, in the corporate world, leaders tend to drive their team with enthusiasm. Pursuit of short term goals with enthusiasm seems to be a style when dealing with lower and middle-level management. But in higher-level management, according to this 'success mantra' one has to focus on long-term goals. When in pursuit of long-term goals, setbacks and short-term failures are inevitable. Sacking capable people over these setbacks does not seem to make sense under his leadership. According to Mr. Anonymous, an underachievement must be followed by training and improvement of skill sets to give it one more improvised try."

Basically, in the corporate world, for higher-level management it is important to nurture *Sattva* to inculcate perseverance.

Looking forward to the secret of nurturing *Gunas* by conscious discipline, we continued to read in silence.

The aspirant should learn not to waste his energy trying to attain the objects of pleasure. Such activity robs one of his core strength, which is the very basis of human advancement and evolution. The aspirant should abstain from activities that preoccupy him with the sense of enjoyment. When he or she is able to tame and keep the *Tamas* and *Rajas* under control he starts to cultivate the *Sattva* quality. This is easier said than done! Adapting to a conscious lifestyle can only tame the *Tamas* and *Rajas* in one's life.

To nurture a certain *Guna* one has to discipline his or her lifestyle. One needs to discipline one's internal lifestyle and also external lifestyle. Internal discipline includes dietary intake and thoughts. External discipline includes recreational activities and maintaining a daily routine.

The aspirant should not make too much effort to change his or her lifestyle. Forced change can only be temporary, and can only last a few years. Here, to discipline one's lifestyle means inculcating habits as a way of living. Permanent change can only happen if one's own thoughts govern the change. There has to be a paradigm shift. This shift can only come with awareness – awareness of knowledge and Self.

I am trying to give awareness of knowledge in this compilation. It is only when one finds logic and has belief in the theory of *Trigunas*, can he think of nurturing them consciously. Awareness of Self is stimulated by following the disciplines and by practicing meditation and contemplation. So the first step is to become aware and contemplate over the philosophy of *Trigunas*. Rest will follow effortlessly. Internal and external disciplines are triggers, they help stimulate the process and avoid slips in the path of nurturing.

"Hey, I totally agree!" Neha exclaimed. *"When people tend to work on the external circumstances to change them they forget the fact that external circumstances are just a manifestation of the internal thoughts, 'The aspirant should not make too much effort to change his or her lifestyle. Forced change can only be temporary, forced change can only last a few years. Here to discipline one's lifestyle means inculcating habits as a way of living. This permanent change can only happen if ones own thoughts govern the change,"* she read out aloud out of the bunch of papers.

Since I stay in a joint family of ten, my father gave me some words of wisdom when my elder brother got married. I suddenly remembered that conversation and wanted to share it with Neha. I told her the back ground and started to quote my dad. He said "Now that the family members are going to increase, you need to remember that your relationship with your brother and *bhabi* will exactly be a manifestation of your true feeling towards them. So, if at all you feel a cold relation with any family member, all you need to do is change your thoughts and feeling towards him or her and you will see magic happening in just a weeks time." I remember following his advice and slowly it became a habit. The blessing of his advice is that I still share love and compassion with nine others in the family

Neha reiterated, "The only way to nurture a Gunas is to first believe in the concept, I remember reading during my course studies that like *Ayurveda* is for the wellness of our physical health, *Trigunas* is for our mental and spiritual well being."

I queried, "What if our internal thoughts are not aligned to our external actions due to whatever reasons?" Neha was quick to reply because of her education, "Such conflicts between thought and action give rise to diseases known as Psychosomatic disorders." "Yes, I have heard that term in relation to mental imbalances giving rise to physical symptoms. This can be as common as sweating because of fear or high blood pressure because of mental stress and anxiety," I simplified. Neha facilitated the topic back to *Trigunas* and said, "Even forcing action in contrary to the tendencies of the *Guna* can lead to Psychosomatic diseases. What Mr. Anonymous is advising us is to nurture habits if we really believe in them and not under any temporary influence."

I confessed, "To me this centuries old knowledge of *Trigunas* makes sense. To my mind its totally worth a try." Our conversation reiterated our conviction, we moved ahead to learn the disciplines of nurturing *Trigunas*.

Over enthusiasm is the enemy of perseverance.

CHAPTER TEN

INTERNAL DISCIPLINE

Internal Discipline – Aahaar (diet) and Vichaar (thoughts)

According to the ancient scriptures, creation is explained by two philosophies: Duality and Non-Duality. Non-Duality states all origin is from Brahman and it is the Brahman that is the cause of *Purush* (soul) and *Prakriti* (nature). Duality states that creation originates with the existence of *Purush* and *Prakriti*.

Samkhya philosophy in particular states that there are two planes of existence: the *Prakriti* and the *Purush*. It is when *Prakriti* comes in contact with *Purush*, that it manifests into existence i.e. living beings. Every part of us except the soul is made of *Prakriti*. Namely, our gross body, subtle body and causal body, are all made up of *Prakriti* and are returned by means of rituals after death. *Prakriti* i.e nature is made up of *Gunas*. The *Gunas* in nature are in potent form of manifestation. The *Gunas* in nature are the source of *Gunas* in living beings. In other words, our mind and body are made up of *Gunas*.

Like energy, *Guna* can neither be created nor destroyed; they are only transformed from one state to another. So as human beings, we can choose which *Gunas* we want to nurture by coming in contact with the *Prakriti* selectively. Conscious nurturing of *Gunas* can be done by choosing what we feed ourselves and also by inculcating the right thoughts.

Aahaar (Food)

Everything we eat has *Gunas* in potent form. Hence food can be categorised as *Sattvik*, *Rajasik* and *Tamasik*. *Sattvik* food is clear and easy to digest, like fresh fruits and vegetables. *Rajasik* food is spicy and pungent, like onions and chicken. Digestion of *Rajasik* food requires more effort and agitates the digestive system. *Tamasik* food is fermented, stale and hard to breakdown. Also, some *Tamasik* consumables are intoxicating.

What to eat?

The type of food determines the type of mind. As food, so the mind; as mind, so the man. Eat easily digestive food i.e. *Sattvik* food. Only a little *Rajasik* food may be consumed. *Rajasik* food is difficult to digest and leaves one in an agitated state of mind. *Tamasik* food is unnatural and stale and therefore leads to lethargy. It should be avoided.

Sattvik Food	Rajasik Food	Tamasik Food
Cereals	Unseasonal Vegetables	Processed and Artificial Food
Wheat	Onions	Frozen Food
Bajra	Salt	Stale Food
Unpolished Rice	Hot Spices	Tobacco
Corn	Sugar	Alcohol
Jowar	Curd	Canned Food
Dals	Fresh meat	Deep-fried Food

Internal Discipline

Sattvik Food	Rajasik Food	Tamasik Food
Fresh Vegetables	Garlic	
Tomatoes	Green chillies	
Turmeric	Fish	
Milk	Cheese	
Butter		
Cardamom		
Cumin Seeds (*Jeera*)		
Coriander Powder (*Dhaniya*)		
Honey		
Jaggery		
Pulses		
Rice Oil		
Groundnut Oil		
Ghee		

As mentioned above, *Gunas* can transform themselves from one to the other by the way they are treated before being consumed. Green vegetables when deep-fried in oil have the tendency to become *Tamasik*. Green vegetables when frozen or canned can also become *Tamasik*.

Eating styles and habits also affect *Gunas*. While eating, one should chew the food properly and enjoy its subtle tastes. One can also indulge in polite conversation that brings joy and happiness. Avoid watching TV. One should go beyond likes and dislikes and not have negative opinions about food. Saying grace before eating does help in attaining the above-mentioned state of mind.

How much to eat?

Moderation is the word. Eat food for sustenance, and eat only as much as will make you hungry after four hours. The stomach gets swollen due to overeating and always demands food in excess. The stomach should be half-filled with food, one-fourth with water, and one-fourth should be left empty for the proper digestion of food and formation of gases. Water should be avoided during meals and should be taken half-an-hour before or after meals.

As the old saying goes, *have breakfast like a king, lunch like a prince and dinner like a pauper*. The explanation for the same is mentioned in *Ayurveda*. As the sun rises, our digestive system gets active; the effectiveness of the digestive system decreases as the sun sets. So dinner should be light and preferably consumed by 7 pm.

If you are not hungry at meal times due to stress, etc. then take some liquids like soup, buttermilk, fruits or salads. Some discipline and regularity regarding food must be maintained. Ideally in a day one should have three meals and one snack time.

As mentioned in the above list, excessive consumption of onions manifests *Rajasik Guna* of action and aggression. The main ingredients in North Indian cuisine are tomatoes and onions, while onions are scarcely used in South Indian cuisine. It is a known fact that the North Indians are an aggressive lot when compared to South Indians. Freshly cooked rice is *Sattvik* but cooked rice kept in water overnight, as they do in South India on weekends, becomes *Tamasik* – this practice makes Sundays more leisurely.

Vichaar (thoughts)

This compilation is an attempt to increase awareness and it is only awareness that can bring the right thought. Thought converts itself to action. Conscious action will lead to a discipline in *Aahaar*, *Vihaar* and *Achaar*. The origin of any course of action is thought.

This practice is nurturing of the right thought. Time and again, different studies have shown that people with depressive, agitated or negative thoughts are more prone to heart diseases. Certain thoughts of fear or agitation make a person sweat or shiver. Which means, thoughts have a direct impact on the physical body.

Facial expressions are an imprint of one's state of mind. A *Sattvik* person will have a pleasant and composed face whereas the same person, when under the influence of the *Rajasik Guna* will have an agitated, uncomfortable look. It can also be analysed vice versa. An agitated uncomfortable person will take decisions under delusion and will not have clarity of thought. A decision taken under the influence of *Rajasik Guna* will reduce productivity and effectiveness on the whole when compared to productivity under the *Sattvik Guna*.

The great English poet, John Milton, has said that, "The mind in its own place can make a heaven of a hell or a hell of a heaven". This is the influence of *Vichaar*.

Sattvik **Thoughts**	*Rajasik* **Thoughts**	*Tamasik* **Thoughts**
Faith	Aggression	Procrastination
Love	Anger	Lethargy
Compassion	Extreme Passion	Laziness
Contentment	Criticism	Sleepiness
Restraint	Dissatisfaction	
Confidence	Anxiety	
Praise	Excitement	
Determination	Sadness	
Contemplation	Fear	

There is a funny annecdote to elaborate on this fact:

A man travelling through a jungle, stands under a tree and wishes for some water to drink. Suddenly, water is available. He realises that this must be the mythological wish-fulfilling tree. He tests the tree and asks for something to eat. Immediately, some food appears. Now he is very certain that he is under the great wish-fulfilling tree. This gets him excited (a *Rajasik* thought). With excitement comes fear and he thinks, 'Suppose a tiger was to come here!' Immediately, the tiger appears. Seeing the tiger he loses control of his thoughts and fears 'the tiger will eat him' and the tiger eats him.

It is important to inculcate *Sattvik* thoughts. Remaining calm and composed can become a habit instead of a reaction. Do not be a slave of circumstances by reactive thinking.

This story depicts how anger or fear leads to delusion of mind. A deluded mind looses discriminatory power and reasoning. Lack of reasoning leads to imbalanced thinking. Thus begins the downfall of a person.

Sattvik thoughts can be inculcated by:

1. Avoid immediate reaction to agitating circumstances. Take a few minutes or overnight before reacting.
2. Avoid criticising others.
3. Do not be judgmental of others. Being judgmental can become a habit and feeds the ego.
4. Try and indulge in charity as it inculcates composure and empathy.
5. Be aware of the tone and pitch of your voice while speaking.

Internal Discipline

6. Breathe right. A breath inhaled with full lung capacity breeds *Sattvik* thoughts of calmness and contentment. Rapid short breaths taken in with half-lung capacity breeds *Rajasik* thoughts of agitation. Breathlessness breeds *Tamasik* thoughts. A dog has rapid breaths, can be easily agitated and has a short life span.

This part was relevant to our day-to-day lives. I could sense Neha analysing the food habits at home. Although we had the external discipline translated in our hands, we opted to take a break and assimilate what we had read. The lady had to take the lead, after all her kitchen was under the scanner. Mr. Anonymous had just accomplished what I could never have dared to do! He just put the kitchen up for judgment. I realised I still could not dare to judge! So I waited without uttering a word.

Taking it in her stride, Neha said, "It is confusing! Mr. Anonymous talks about the onion eating habit of North Indians with as much authority as he talks about the *Tamasik* habit of South Indians to keep cooked rice overnight to facilitate a lethargic Sunday. His intricate knowledge of both cuisines causes confusion regarding his own origin. I wonder whether he is South Indian or North Indian!"

I pointed out, "He could also mention the popular North Indian Sunday brunch of *puris* and *bhaturas*, deep fried in oil to facilitate the leisurely holiday nap. Weekday meals seem *Rajasik* or *Sattvik* all over geographies but on Sunday it seems the *Tamasik* food habit are universally designed to enjoy the blissful lethargy."

"Fear, anger, agitation are all *Rajasik* thoughts, chicken and other meat also nurture *Rajas*," I pointed out. Neha awaited the connection as I continued, "When an animal is being killed, he exhibits fear, anger and agitation. According to Mr. Anonymous, *Thoughts of fear and agitation make a person sweat or shiver. Which means thoughts have a direct impact on the physical body.*"

I read out from the *Triguna Mantra* and continued my thought, "An animal, when being killed to eat, oozes out biological chemicals linked to fear, anger and agitation. This meat when consumed passes the same attributes of anger, fear and agitation to the human body. After consumption of this *Rajasik* food by us, these attributes manifest themselves through us, in the real world. So the connection between what we eat and our thoughts and action seems clear."

Neha pointed out, "Determination is mentioned under *Sattvik* thought and passion is mentioned as a *Rajasik* thought, although they seem to be linked. A passionate pursuit will often be similar to a determined pursuit." After a few seconds of thoughtful silence she continued, "A passionate pursuit has a major quotient of emotion in it which probably makes it *Rajasik*, whereas a determined pursuit indicates focus."

Merely altering the feeling within, can amend cold relations with any person.

CHAPTER ELEVEN

EXTERNAL DISCIPLINE

External Discipline – Vihaar (Recreational Activites) and Achar (Routine)

Vihaar **(Recreation)**

Repetition of thoughts is a major issue with many people. Statistically, more than 90 percent of thoughts in a day are the same as the previous day. Having the same thought repeatedly causes attachment to that thought. Attachment to it adds an emotional quotient during the process of execution. A positive result leads to excitement and a negative result leads to anger or depression. All these emotions are *Rajasik* in nature. Anger, excitement or depression lead to delusion, thus lowering the ability of taking the right decisions. An aspirant should thus avoid repetition of thoughts.

Vihaar or recreational activity calms the mind and also avoids repetition of thoughts. One can choose recreational activities like sports, singing, learning music or art. It helps maintain calmness and composure, thus inculcating the *Sattvik Guna*.

Maintaining good relationships in the family and society also plays an important role in one's over all well-being.

Achar (**Routine**)

In the first step, the aspirant reaches the source of knowledge. Then he tries to assimilate as much knowledge as he can. After contemplation on what he has assimilated, some thoughts get completely accepted by his mind. It is important that if certain habits/thoughts make sense to an aspirant, he must include them in his daily routine. This may require certain change in the lifestyle of an aspirant. Maintaining a routine is merely inculcating these habits in one's lifestyle.

One popular dialogue that all of us have heard from our friends and family is 'I am dieting to reduce weight'. How many times have we seen it work effectively? Even if that person reduces weight he tends to regain it within the same year. More often than not, a crash diet leads to physical complications, such as a pain or swelling in the joints or depression. These complications occur because of deficiency of some vitamin or the other. Dieting is not something that should be done for a specific time period, rather, having a good diet has to become a part of one's lifestyle.

Sticking to one's meal, sleep and exercise daily is of the utmost importance in order to have a healthy *Sattvik* mind. To keep the *Sattva* dominant, it is necessary to discipline oneself and limit pleasure seeking. This is done by external discipline.

Gunas can be looked at from another perspective. In the Bhagwad Gita, Chapter 14 Verses 21, 22, 23, Arjuna asks Shri Krishna the characteristics of the three *Gunas*. Krishna explains that the predominance of a particular *Guna* has a paradigm shift in the mind. An individual sees the world differently in accordance to the predominant *Guna*. Every individual has a particular wavelength that determines what he connects to and how he perceives it.

As the TV set responds to TV waves, a radio set to radio waves and a mobile set to mobile waves, a set of *Gunas* only responds to the waves of their own wavelength. Thus the resonances of our *Gunas* govern our actions and reactions. *Gunas* determine our resonance or connect with food, people, things and even places. This explains the fact that by nurturing a certain set of *Gunas* the results are a natural offshoot and seem effortless.

As mentioned earlier, *Gunas* are dynamic and the proportion in which they exist may change over different phases of life. Therefore, nurturing *Gunas* with consistency avoids fluctuations and helps declutter the mind, thereby enhancing clarity of thought. One strong *Guna* will connect with similar sets of thoughts and the weakness of the other two *Gunas* will avoid unnecessary thoughts to enter the mind, thereby increasing the focus of an individual. Changing the predominant *Guna* brings about a paradigm shift of the mind. An individual will always be able to justify his behaviour and actions because under the influence of 'his proportion of *Gunas*' he is connecting to the world in a certain unique way and that is his righteous, justified way.

In criminal psychoanalysis it has been observed that a criminal while performing a crime, say shoplifting, is aware that he is performing an anti-social activity. A shoplifter commits the crime under the influence of his *Gunas* although he is aware of his wrongdoing. He is merely acting under the influence of his *Gunas*. The *Rajas* in him is dominant and is supported by *Tamas*.

I was born into a non-vegetarian family and have enjoyed eating meat for 34 years. But now I am a vegetarian. Although I am cognizant to the fact that the non-vegetarian dish in front of me is a great preparation and is mouthwatering to any meat eater, I cannot eat it. This sounds ironic but it is true. I have nurtured my *Gunas*

External Discipline

in such a proportion that my *Gunas* cannot connect or resonate to the vibes given out by the otherwise skillfully prepared dish. So I know that it's a treat but cannot eat it because of the paradigm shift. Being a vegetarian is not self-restraint but a paradigm shift because of a set of consciously nurtured *Gunas*.

A person with *Rajasik* predominance gets attracted to pleasure objects/activities like spicy food, latest cars, loud rock or foot-tapping music. On the other hand, a person with the predominance of *Sattvik Guna* inherently starts enjoying fresh green vegetables, soothing calm music, and spiritual places. The predominant *Guna* starts responding to the vibes of its symptoms. So one needs to only make an effort to nurture the right *Guna* and make it predominant. Thereafter, the *Guna* and its tendencies nurture each other and it becomes a lifestyle unless some major shakeup happens. It is important to be aware or rather make an effort to remove the veil of ignorance from the mind.

To choose one's circumstances is also a way to nurture and cultivate a particular *Guna*. If I want to feel upbeat on a particular evening and have my *Rajas Guna* dominate the other two, I will choose to go to a place with lively music. When I am feeling confused and restless and want to calm down and relax i.e. nurture the *Sattvik Guna*, I shall plan my evening with soft and calming music with serene ambience. The right kind of symptom can enhance the *Guna*.

All this sounds obvious. The ideal lifestyle is obvious. There is always a gap between the ideal and the actual lifestyle. It is general human tendency to move towards the ideal lifestyle but one tends to do so by lowering the ideal towards the actual under the pretext of practicality. Practicality is conveniently used to bridge and justify the gap between ideal and actual. It is an inherent human tendency to aspire towards an ideal lifestyle. The endeavour should be to take the actual as close as possible to the ideal. The results become an offshoot of the lifestyle and seem effortless.

The point is, are we aware of this cause and effect phenomenon. Do we choose our circumstances or lifestyle keeping in mind the *Guna* that we want to nurture? Most of us are just sucked into circumstances without awareness or under peer pressure. We get sucked into an evening with *Tamasik* food, tagging it as a stressbuster, thereby feeling lethargic the next morning. We are unaware of the fact that they are obvious *Tamasik* symptoms of our lifestyle. Our senses will always be lured into *Tamasik* and *Rajasik* circumstances since these circumstances feed the senses. That's when our awareness needs to step in and decide which *Guna* do we want to nurture.

Circumstances that nurture *Rajas*:

1. Competitive environments or activity.
2. Loud/foot tapping music or dancing.
3. Table thumping and aggressive conversations.
4. Vibrant colours in attire or surroundings.
5. Choice of friends and companions with *Rajasik* attributes.

Circumstances that nurture *Sattva*:

1. Calming and serene music
2. Long walks in fresh air.
3. Visits to temples, churches, mosques and other spiritual places.

4. Spending some time alone in contemplation and awareness.
5. Choice of friends and companions with *Sattvik* attributes.
6. Indulging in calming conversations with like-minded people.
7. Reading books of wisdom.

Circumstances that nurture *Tamas*:

1. Late nights, dark ambiance and sleeping till late in the morning.
2. Intoxication.
3. Choice of friends and companions with *Tamasik* attributes.

While I was writing this I was asked:

In Europe, China, Middle East or Africa, where their basic food is meat, how does *Aahaar* play a role in their nurturing of *Gunas*? Wise men with attributes of pure *Sattva* evolve from across geographies.

After much research and discussions, I gathered "*Aahar*, though is a component to build our *Gunas*, however, it is not the only thing. Out of the four disciplines *Aahar, Vichaar, Vihar* and *Achar* the strongest influence is of *Vichaar*. A person who is introspective can exhibit symptoms of any Guna thereby overriding the effects of other disciplines. So a meat eating aspirant with awareness and introspection can exhibit *sattvik* attributes. But an aspirant with *sattvik Aahaar* habits and *Tamasik*

Vichaar can never exhibit *Sattvik* attributes. *Vichaar* has the most powerful influence. Although all the four disciplines in alignment can make the nurturing effortless and delightful.

Kahlil Gibran, a Poet and Philosopher from the Middle East shared his views about the tradition of eating meat in the region in his compilation, *The Prophet*. When asked to speak about eating habits, he started with a wish... 'It would have been great if you could live on the fragrance of the earth or be sustained by light. But since you must kill to eat and rob the newlyborn of its mother's milk to quench your thirst, let it then be an act of worship. When you slay a beast say to him in your heart:

 "By the same power that slays you, I too am slain; and I too shall be consumed.

For the law that delivered you into my hand shall deliver me into a mightier hand."

In my experiential learning over years, I have noticed that as the *Sattva* grows to become predominant, the awareness increases. One becomes sensitive of the changes that happen to the body and mind. The ill-effects of overeating or extreme austerities are consciously avoided. One is able to find a natural balance in all aspects of life and is not lured by overindulgence in sensual pleasures. This sensitivity and balance leads to mastery over body, mind and senses, thus leading to freedom from disease and disturbances of the mind.

Another interesting point of view came out in a discussion:

Food is not only what we eat. This aspect is only food for our Body. As discussed earlier, whatever we take in through our five senses is also *Aahaar*. In fact, they are food for our Mind. Therefore, other than food that we eat,

External Discipline

the influence of contents taken through five senses also nourish our mind. In other countries, though they may consume meat, etc. their mind is being fed by *Sattvik* thoughts.

"Wow, now that can be a life changer!" Neha exclaimed. "The insight on repeated thoughts as mentioned under external discipline is also mentioned in the Gita." She went to our room, pulled out a commentary on Gita and read out Shloka 2.62, 2.63. "As a person contemplates on the object of the senses, there arises in him attachment to them; from attachment arises desire; from desire anger is produced. From anger comes delusion; from delusion the loss of memory; from the disappearance of memory, the loss of faculty of discrimination; by loss of the faculty of discrimination one perishes."

"Mr. Anonymous must be a well-read person!" She concluded with a smile. I read the thought behind her smile. She seemed to be indicating towards my cozy corner reading habit and my visits to the library. Oh my god! Unconsciuosly, I had probably found my mentor!

Further justifying the query that Mr. Anonymous had very clearly explained, I shared an insight with Neha. The other day I had taken the Airport Express to Connaught Place in Delhi and found myself sitting next to a Buddhist Monk. I asked him about his views on vegetarianism and to my surprise he replied, "There is nothing specific but as a practice we do not get non-vegetarian food into our residential monasteries."

"Why this irony?" I asked.

He replied, "We believe in meditation to increase our control on the mind. As monks we have to knock on 7 doors a day and ask for *bhiksha* i.e. food from the householders. We eat only what is given to us from those seven door knocks." He reiterated, "We are not supposed to knock on the eighth door. Under this discipline, we have to respect what has been given to us and consume it without discrimination."

Now this was a clear case of conscience overriding the influence of *Aahaar*. The fact that they are not supposed to get meat in their monastery reflects their preferences. At the same time, they honour whatever is given to them in the form of *bhiksha*. The discipline of the mind to be unattached to *Aahaar*, overrides the influence of what they actually consume.

This brings to light another interesting statement by Mr. Anonymous: *'It is important to be aware or rather to remove the veil of ignorance from the mind.'* All the above mentioned discipline suddenly seems to be more of working on the mind rather than anything else. The process of 'being aware' and 'removing the veil of ignorance' has a peculiar relationship between them. It is like the relationship between light and darkness. To remove darkness from a room one cannot take the darkness out of the room and throw it away. To remove the darkness from the room the only way is to bring in light. Similarly to remove ignorance from the mind the only way is to bring in knowledge and awareness.

Subsequently, dad, our urdu script translator, informed us that the next few pages were on the dissection of the mind according to the scriptures. In order to study medical science, one has to dissect the body. Similarly, it seems, to study philosophy it is important to dissect the subtle aspect of the mind according to the scriptures.

My trip to the Kumbh was also round the corner now; Neha promised to wait for me to resume our sessions. We asked dad as to how many more pages were left with him since a new inquisitiveness had set in now. In fact, I was determined to meet Mr. Anonymous. I had enough information about him and was sure my detective instincts would surely be able to find him.

Like energy, *Gunas* can neither be created nor destroyed; they are only transformed from one state to another.

CHAPTER TWELVE

AMITABH BACHCHAN - A CASE STUDY

I was looking forward to meeting personalities from different walks of life who had taken a trip to attend the largest congregation of people with common interest. Kumbh *Mela* is also known for its display of mystic endeavours of *Tapaswis*. The austerities and mystic display pull a lot of people with the feeling of reverence and curiosity.

My train was to leave at 5 o' clock and I was booked in the First AC compartment for an 18-hour journey. As I boarded the train from New Delhi Railway Station I could sense a common purpose amongst the passengers. Almost all the people in the train were headed for the Kumbh *Mela*. I was reminded of the statistics – 120 million people expected to visit this humongous *Mela* to experience 40 days of glory.

I went into my cabin, made myself comfortable on my berth. Travelling alone and expecting the unexpected, I had packed light; a small backpack to facilitate walking was all I had. I knew there was a lot of walking in store, as the *Mela* was spread across 30 acres of land with no transportation inside. I was prepared to walk to every nook and corner of the *Mela* and wanted to explore as much in my three days stay.

The Millennium City Hermit

As the train started, I exchanged pleasantries with my three co-passengers, who were all, surprisingly, around my age. It seems that the age of acknowledging spirituality was reducing. It seemed paradoxical that in this progressive era of science and technology, youngsters were treading the journey to discover mysticism, austerities and spirituality.

I was on the upper berth; the other upper berth was taken by Kapil, who seemed to be in his thirties. He appeared to be fit and agile by the way he climbed to make himself comfortable. He seemed to be a cricket buff – he was engrossed in hearing live cricket commentary on his radio transistor and his expressions were revealing as the game progressed. He pumped his hand over a boundary, and it made a huge thud on the roof, which brought smiles to the rest in the cabin.

The smiles helped us break the ice among the rest and soon we got talking. The two births below were occupied by Vimal and Clyde, an American based out of Hong Kong. Vimal was in his forties, belonged to a small town in Madhya Pradesh, a central state in India. He seemed non-pretentious, as his smile graduated to giggles over Kapil's thuds and sighs. The cabin was soon filled by an aroma, as Vimal could not resist digging into the *puris* and mango pickle that he was carrying. For a minute, I got worried – I had not brought anything to eat on this long journey. I walked towards the pantry and confirmed – the meals were to be served on the train.

Clyde had flown in from Hong Kong to visit the *Mela*. To our surprise, he seemed to be relishing the *puri* and pickle combo. He soon revealed that he was Yoga regular and was exposed to various pickles generously shared after the morning class with fellow Indians.

As we got talking, Clyde stated that he was expecting company of senior citizens on this journey. Kapil, who had by now removed his earplugs and was part of the conversation, responded that he was looking forward to exploring the areas that were little known to him. He acknowledged the mysticism attached to the *Mela* and the staunch belief of the people that could not be explained. He claimed to be researching the mystics and finding answers to explain them.

Clyde expressed, "I am here to experience the lesser known styles of existence."

Kapil continued with an enriching wisdom on mystics, "The apple that fell on Newton was not the first one that ever fell. It was the first that got noticed and got elaborated into theory of gravity. If the occurrences of the universe or nature would wait for being researched first, it would be a mess. The apple would never have fallen before the derivation of the theory of gravity. Phenomenon and mystics will occur; it is our ignorance or the lack of knowledge that hamper our beliefs and make us myopic." The cricket buff seemed to be quite thoughtful!

Kapil's modesty and thought earned appreciation. His flow of thought did not stop here as he continued, "Usually, we have such a myopic view that we think the truth of our comprehension is the real truth. Our ego makes us believe in the truth of our comprehension rather than trying to expand our view to comprehend the real truth. Our limited comprehension seems to be the truth and we never explore further to increase its scope. Our arrogance usually attempts to assert our understanding on others."

I realised, this train had a lot of thoughtful people and this journey itself would be an insightful one. The thoughts seemed heavier than the otherwise fit people. Enriching conversations, mysticism and austerities of the *sadhus*, temporary infrastructure on the banks of river Ganga to support 120 million devotees in 40 days and lots more was in store for this trip.

While the journey continued, we were getting privileged treatment by the staff in the first AC carriage. We felt like goats being fed before taken to the butcher. The royal treatment was in sharp contrast to the austere means we would be exposed to in the next few days.

While Kapil was a cricket buff, Vimal seemed to be a Bollywood movie freak and Clyde was a thorough reader of Indian history and scriptures. I expressed my interest in the *Triguna* and got a very participatory response from everybody. Most of us in the cabin had a lifestyle in alignment with conscious nurturing of the *Gunas*. All were well read and had a thorough knowledge on the subject. Legendary names and their attributes were getting linked to their lifestyles and *Gunas*. Just then, Vimal came out with a name that drew even Clyde's attention: Amitabh Bachchan. The kind of knowledge Vimal had about the legendary actor seemed as though he had been Amitabh's immediate neighbour throughout his life.

He started off from the early times and incidents in Mr. Bachchan's life and linked them very effortlessly with *Trigunas*. Vimal and Amitabh seemed to have grown up together although Vimal was in his forties and Mr. Bachchan was in his seventies. Even in his seventies, Amitabh oozed energy and was constantly reinventing himself. His career graph was reaching new crests every year. Usually careers peak in during the forties but Amitabh was rewriting the formulae.

Vimal reminded us that Amitabh had gone through many a phases. He had an early stint of struggle in Kolkata. In the beginning, Amitabh landed himself a couple of sales jobs. He participated in talent hunts but was rejected. He also failed English and Hindi tests for the post of a News Announcer for All India Radio. He tasted success in the late 1970s followed by a near-death experience and also bankruptcy thereafter.

His first break came in the form of a role in *Saat Hindutani*, released in 1970. Amitabh also did a few radio jingles and was paid Rs. 50 for each jingle. In the late 70's, with hit movies like Sholay, Kabhie Kabhie, Don, Trishul he became a rage.

All these phases of failures and successes must have had an effect on his set of *Gunas*. I remember Mr. Anonymous mentioning that the proportion of *Gunas* can change with a change in lifestyle and also due to major shake-ups in one's life. After hearing about Amitabh Bachchan's roller coaster ride, he seemed to qualify as a case study for the latter reason as well. The shake-ups in his life definitely would have had an effect on his *Gunas*.

In the 80's, Amitabh was out of business for almost five years because of an injury while shooting for the movie *Coolie*. It was a near-death experience for him. After the injury, he was unwell with myasthenia gravis followed by an accident in which he had burnt his hand. After the death of Prime Minister Indira Gandhi in 1984, he got pulled into politics because of his popularity and proximity to Rajiv Gandhi. However, he got very uncomfortable in politics and exited soon.

For an established onscreen performer to vanish for five years is like writing an obituary for his career. After the five-year break he tried to make a comeback but did not bag any interesting movies. He then tried to corporatise the film industry and launched a company by the name of AB Corp. This decision boomeranged and left him with a pile of liabilities worth nearly Rs. 800-900 million. Gradually, he did make a comeback and paid off all his liabilities.

During this topsy-turvy phase of success and failures he became a teetotaler, a vegetarian and also quit smoking. All through the phase he kept telling himself that this too shall pass.

All these phases in the life of a now legendary success story makes it interesting to study the change in *Gunas* during his lifetime. I thought Vimal was a lethal combination with knowledge of *Gunas* and intricate knowledge of the life of a legend. If he can join the dots of Amitabh's phases to his *Aahaar, Vichaar, Aachaar* and *Vihaar* it would be extremely insightful. It would be interesting to know how Amitabh reacted in various circumstances, especially during the tough times. My keen interest gave Vimal an opportunity to tell us more about Amitabh's life in the light of *Trigunas* and *Dincharya*.

Interestingly, all through the growing years Shri Harivansh Rai Bachchan and Shrimati Teji Bachchan used to take Amitabh and Ajitabh, his elder brother, for early morning walks by the Sangam in Allahabad. They enjoyed the sight of sunrise followed by bathing in the holy waters and a breakfast of milk and *jalebis*. A routine like that is most likely to nurture *Sattvik* traits. Coincidentally, we were also heading for the same bathing point, the Sangam in Allahabad.

Amitabh claims to have lived a very mediocre student life, always striving to rise beyond. He did achieve second prize in long jump at Sherwood and Kendall Cup for acting. Further in college, he bagged a small role in the Miranda House performance of Benn Levy's theatre show. His striving efforts reflect *Rajasik-Sattvik* attitude.

Vimal even remembered that in an interview with Khalid Mohamed, when Amitabh was asked about his training in the Amateur Theatre group in Kolkata, he said "No, it wasn't a training ground. It was just a joy of indulging in an extracurricular activity, enacting the written word or even taking in the smell of the stage floor" – *Sattva* statement. He continued, "It was the pleasure of evoking applause and the pain of enduring the hooting and catcalls" – *Rajas* statement.

Amitabh landed himself a job in Kolkata and was enjoying his freedom and paycheques. He reached a four-digit salary of Rs. 1000 per month. The Filmfare Madhuri Talent contest winners were being promised a monthly salary of Rs. 2,500 with an assurance of a subsequent raise to as much as Rs. 5,000. The wishful increase in salary drove him to enter the contest but in vain. This attempt signifies that he was action-oriented and also reflects *Kamya Karma*, which is a trait of *Rajas*.

He tends to symbolise his achievements by mentioning the list of cars that he bought from the beginning of his career. From a Black Morris Minor to a Standard Herald when he was working in Kolkata with Bird and Company and later Blacker and Company. These phases in Kolkata were followed by a stint with no car during his struggling years in Mumbai. Then again, he started doing well in films and bought a Fiat, moved on to Pontiac and then to a Mercedes-Benz. Around

1976 he built his own house 'Prateeksha'. He felt overwhelmed during the construction of his new bungalow and decided to spend a night on the bare floor of his house even before its completion. Amitabh seemed to have enjoyed recognition and also the fruits of success in these phases.

Enjoying recognition and fruits of success is inherent to any human being. What's important is the perspective and the drive behind doing work. Working for acquiring materialistic possessions reflects *Kamya Karma*, thus *Rajas*. Working with a drive to do a good job and then acquiring materialistic possession as a result of the fruits of work reflects *Kartavya Karma*, thus *Sattvik*. After acquisition of the materialistic possessions, if one tends to flaunt it or feed his ego, it means he is slipping into *Rajas*. Even though one might have done *Kartavya Karma* for achieving success, one might not be aware of doing so.

Often one is not exposed to the material world and is involved in dedicated and disciplined work. This *Kartavya Karma* brings success but soon after being exposed to the material world the doer gets attached to it and starts to work for more material acquisitions. This phenomenon of slipping from *Sattvik* to *Rajasik* after getting exposed to the material world is not uncommon.

Repeatedly in his interviews, Amitabh has admitted to being a pessimist and dealing with insecurity. Despite achieving tremendous success, never has he exhibited an iota of arrogance. He has never acknowledged any piece of his work as outstanding; he tends to believe his work has always been mediocre. He is always open to suggestion on improvising his shot, even from his make-up man or spot boys behind the cameras. All this is hard to believe, but after an exhaustive question-answer session with Vimal, I had to believe in the legend's extraordinary humility.

Vimal continued to narrate more incidents, "In the 1970s, when Amitabh had a brief stint living with his brother Ajitabh in Mumbai and tasted success, he did get swayed into heavy duty partying. The change of cars and partying hard with his group of friends including Zeenat Aman and Sheila Jones during a successful phase reflects *Rajas*."

Amitabh has gone through many a phases. Early stints of struggle to tasting success in the late '70s and early '80s to a break because of an injury while shooting for Coolie, then back to a struggling period followed by legendary achievements. This periodic in-an-out of business due to circumstances, made him insecure and a fear of uncertainties seemed to have crept in. Although he has acknowledged his love for theatre, the fear of uncertainties forbids him to take time out and risk his successful cinematic career path. This uncertainty is an outcome of his attachment to the success in cinema. The *Rajas* attribute of attachment is due to major shake-ups in his career.

Amitabh makes an interesting notation while appreciating Hrishikesh Mukerjee's direction. Vimal quoted Amitabh, "In modern day cinema we've lost Hrishida's kind of moments of silence and introspection. Today's essence is speed. The attention span of the audience has become short and limited. There's just no time to sit back and reflect." A shift of the audience from *Sattva* to *Rajas* is indicated in this statement. This mass shift from *Sattva* to *Rajas* can be easily observed in our daily lives.

I got reminded of the days when Neha tried to introduce some of the old, evergreen movies like *Chupke Chupke* and *Mughl-e-Azam* to our teen kids. Kids were unable to even complete one movie. I narrated this incident to the others. Clyde pitched in and said, "The sense of appeal is ever changing over generations. The way content has to be packaged to have an appeal depends on the end viewer. As I have moved over continents I see advertisements also need to be changed in different geographies to have an appeal."

The mass shift seemed to have triggered Clyde into the conversation. He continued, "Our lifestyles are now more aligned to nurture *Rajas* thus the stress and tensions. The rage, anger and passionate pursuits have led to broken families and increased desires. All this can be acceptable, provided one learns to live with it in decency. One needs to retain love and compassion and not become brutal and hurtfully aggressive. In my opinion, the *Rajas* is to be tamed by *Sattva*." Clyde's international exposure was insightful.

After Clyde went silent we all shifted our focus towards Vimal again. He quipped, "Relax, I am not a film magazine. I am just another Bachchan fan."

I told him that his intricate knowledge of the legend's lifestyle and phases and the way he could join the dots with the concept of *Triguna* was very helpful, as I was researching the *Triguna* concept."

Vimal took his time and then continued, "During the period of tussle between Amitabh and the media, there was an annual Filmfare Award function held. Practically every other award under the sun went to the film *Deewar*, a superhit starring

Amitabh Bachchan. When it came to the Best Actor's award, Amitabh was called upon the stage to present the trophy to Sanjeev Kumar for *Aandhi*. Every one was of the opinion that Amitabh deserved the trophy! The punishment to Amitabh was pretty obvious. After thirty years of this incident, Amitabh still narrates that he apparently got the loudest applause from the audience that evening while presenting the trophy. He also got a letter from the *Filmfare* editor appreciating his sporting behaviour. The consolation act from the editor and the audience has been on his mind since thirty years. Definitely shows a prominence of *Rajas* during the 1970's."

Vimal seemed to be an encyclopedia for sure. I asked him how he knows so much about Amitabh and he went into a retrospective mood.

"Can you guys believe I have cut a cake and celebrated all his birthdays since my teens?"

Clyde quipped in amazement, "Now here is a die hard fan. I am sure he is into idol worship."

Vimal continued, "The 80's and the early 90's were a long struggle period for Amitabh and the shake-ups changed his mind set and also the set of *Gunas* he had before the struggle. He had already given up meat, alcohol and smoking, thus aligning his eating habits to nurture the *Sattva Guna*.

"He sleeps only for five-six hours a day and wakes up fresh. A *Sattvik* person is detached from his actions and treats most of the situations unemotionally. By doing so, the mind is not fatigued. For the physical body, six hours are enough to take on the next day. The emotions of *Rajas* fatigues the mind i.e. excitement or depression, anger or laughter, sadness or joy. In a *Sattvik* state, the mind remains calm and fresh to take productive decisions and does not need more than five-six hours of sleep to rejuvenate."

The train journey went on with our conversation lasting till 9 pm. Evaluating a legendary personality in different phases of life gave me a lot of clarity on the concept of *Gunas*. We were up early as the train reached Allahabad around 7 am.

**Instead of trying to expand
our comprehension to seek truth,
we often seek solace within
a limited horizon.**

CHAPTER THIRTEEN

KUMBH *MELA*

I was staying in a suburb named Jhoosi, a short walk from the *Mela*. I had a room on the terrace with the basics in place. I had a separate entry and exit that was a necessity as the *Mela* was alive 24 hours. I wanted to experience the *Mela* at all hours of the day and night during my three-day visit.

I freshened up and walked towards the *Mela*. From a point on the bridge I could see kilometers of colourful fabric covering the ground on both sides of the river Ganga. There was not a concrete structure in view. I walked in among an ocean of people moving around. The *Mela* had innumerable *Akharas* or temporary hermitages of the sages. One could walk into any of the hermitage and indulge in meaningful conversations. I walked kilometers and took refuge in a hermitage when I was in no condition to walk any further. There were talks organised for people to hear and understand the scriptures.

There were various kind of sages with interesting pursuits. Some devoted to perform austerities all their lives popularly known as *Tapasvis*. Some sages entered the *Mela* in a cavalry of vehicles with pomp and show. Some sages had devoted their lives to asceticism while others ran huge organisations with cash reserves to reinvest like any other corporate. Some sages had also dedicated their lives in pursuit of Yoga. As per my understanding, I could broadly categorise the sages into three categories – the Ascetics, the Yogis and the Chairmans delivering words of wisdom. It was an interesting walk, after which I decided to go back and come prepared for a dip in the Ganga early next day.

Next morning, at 5 am I was taking a dip in the holy waters of the Ganga enjoying myself to the fullest. Looking at the sunrise while in the water was sanctity personified. The whole view was mesmerising. As I looked to check on my pile of clothes and belongings I realised a man was sitting uncomfortably close to them. I felt a little insecure as I was alone and the pile of clothes had a mobile phone and some cash.

I walked out immediately and started to dry myself with the towel. The man sitting there noticed my insecurity and asked, "Are you seeking security or are you seeking freedom from insecurity?" The question was heavy. I thought to myself, will I want somebody to watch over my valuables as security or would I prefer being free of these valuables while I enjoy my dip? The answer was simple – I would have preferred to come to the banks of Ganga without any valuables so as to be free and enjoy the waters, without getting disturbed by the thought of insecurity.

Looking into my silent face he probably noticed that I was not taking the conversation forward, although in my thoughts I was evaluating what he had said. As he was getting up to go I noticed he had a walking stick by his side. I bent to give him his walking stick.

He thanked me and said, "The more I use this walking stick the more insecure I feel about losing it. My legs are weak and as the Kumbh has to be covered by foot I am using this stick for my comfort. I fear I may continue to use it even after the Kumbh, although I feel a sense of freedom without this stick. Not using the stick might slow me down but at least I can venture into the river without the fear of losing it.

"This wealth, fame, power are all crutches that give you a sense of insecurity and limit your ventures in life. One may accumulate wealth in life but getting attached to it is what gives a sense of insecurity; insecurity because of the fear of losing it. So you want security or you want freedom from insecurity?" he repeated his question.

In the evening I called up home told them that I will not be available on the phone for the next few hours, left my phone, camera, wallet, etc. in the room and kept a 100-rupee note in my pocket and left for the Kumbh again. Leaving my insecurities behind I did feel like a newborn renunciant with nothing to loose. I felt secured within. I ventured deeper into the *Mela* and enjoyed a nice dip in the holy waters. I went around walking, and enjoying the aura created by millions of devotes and sages. I got tired and entered a hermitage to take shelter.

As I entered I seemed to have disturbed a sage who was relaxing inside. He was kind enough to give me space to sit. I noticed he had a lot of Sanskrit texts lying next to him. As we got into a conversation I noticed he was well-versed with the oldest Hindu texts – the *Upanishads*. I asked him about *Trigunas* and he gave me an altogether new perspective. He told me that *Trigunas* were the cosmic (*Prakritic*) origins of creation. The five basic elements i.e. air, water, fire, space and earth are made of the three *Gunas*. Each element has all the three *Gunas* that give them various attributes. The gross form or the tangible look and feel of all the five elements is because of the *Tamas Guna* present in it that makes it inert and gives it a consistent form. If it were not for *Tamas*, the gross form would not have taken shape and the element would keep changing its form constantly.

Our body and the whole nature are made up of these five elements. Our body occupies space, a gross element. There is air throughout the body, oxygen being the basic necessity. Fire gives it body temperature and water gives it shape. The earth is present in the form of minerals and elements like carbon, calcium, etc. our input of *Gunas* comes from our interaction with nature in the form of what we eat, what we see and any other kind of contact with it.

During the Kumbh *Mela*, certain days are earmarked as the days of the 'Royal Dip' or '*Shahi Snaan*'. My third day of the visit was the 10th of February, the most auspicious day for the dip. And the time determined was in the *Brahma Mahurat* i.e. around dawn. My curiosity made my presence inevitable. As I walked in the morning from my dwelling towards the *Mela*, I saw something beyond my comprehension. All roads from the railway stations and bus terminals were swarmed with people walking towards the *Mela*. I later found out, according to official statistics more the 25 million people had taken a dip on that day i.e. more than double the population of Delhi had been present at the *Mela* on a single day!

I suddenly became a part of a crowd stretching for kilometers on the road. This gave me an opportunity to interact with my fellow walkers. I realised that the majority of the people visit the *Mela* to take a dip and gain a direct entry pass to heaven. It is a ritual for them that has been followed through generations. That is what makes it the largest congregation of religious people in the world. *Naga Sadhus* made a grand entry for the dip. Historically the *Nagas* were the warrior clan that took its birth in the times of Adi Shankarachaya. The clan's purpose was to save Hinduism from invasions. I could feel the fierceness as the bare-bodied, ash-covered, long-haired *sadhus* made an entry, dancing in ecstasy. Despite the large number of people, the morning dip was very well organised by the officials including policemen on horses to manage the crowd.

My trip was coming to an end, I made my way back to the train station. The chaos there was a different kind. A horrifying experience of millions of people leaving town after the auspicious dip, all at the same time. I finally made myself comfortable in my seat. My experience of the auspicious dip made me once again appreciate the effort put in to organise the event. As I took a breather, I realised that the trip gave me new experiences and exposures. It was a congregation of ascetics, yogis and corporate chairmans. One had to carve out his own *Mela* within the larger *Mela*. For me it was all about conversations and expansion of my scope of comprehension.

Throughout the return journey my determination to meet the writer of urdu pages grew stronger. I was aching to pull out the first and the last couple of pages that I had kept in my wardrobe. I was sure they would give me enough information to track Mr. Anonymous. His write up was so enriching I could only wait to meet him in person. I wanted to experience his aura. I wanted to know how he imbibed the knowledge of the *Gunas*. How he lives in the real world and what impact did the nurturing of *Gunas* have in the competitive, result-oriented corporate world.

On my return journey I was seated with a group of doctors who were residing in an institute close to Bengaluru in South India. They had done a doctorate in Yoga Therapy and *Panch Karma*. Conversing with them I came to know that the founder of their institute was an ex-NASA scientist. He had returned to India and set up laboratories to scientifically prove the theories mentioned in our scriptures, including the theory of *Trigunas*.

This young group of doctors had finished their PhDs and had stayed back in the institute to research the concepts of *Panch Karma*, Yoga Therapy, *Trigunas*, etc. One of them was involved in making an implicit tool to know the proportion of *Trigunas* in an individual. I asked him what he meant by an implicit tool. He said, "Most of the people who are likely to take this test are aware of the concept of *Trigunas*. As they take the test, subconsciously their answers or reactions are manipulated by their knowledge of the *Gunas*. So I am designing a tool by which even if the person giving the test has complete knowledge of *Trigunas*, shall not be able to manipulate his answers."

I thought to myself, how coincidentally, I have been getting guidance to enhance my knowledge on the topic. All I could do is thank God for setting up the order that was gradually unfolding.

I asked the doctor to relate the *Guna* predominance to the personalities he had encountered in real life. He thought for a while and then spoke, "Every person acts according to the three *Gunas* present in him. People with predominance of *Rajas* or *Tamas* tend to enjoy the worldly pleasures and that also reflects in the their nature and body types." Now that was interesting!

"It has been observed that those people who are dominated by fatty tissues tend to enjoy sensory pleasures," the doctor continued, "Those with dominance of muscular tissues are more action-oriented. People in whom dominance of nervous system is more than fatty and muscular tissues tend to be more contemplative than the action-oriented."

He smiled and said, "Most of us have finished our studies from the institute but are so intrigued that we have chosen to continue our research. Our parents are constantly luring us with marriage proposals by sending us photographs of beautiful, eligible girls. I am sure they have their doubts!" His smile broke into a giggle.

Similar to my journey to Kumbh, the return journey was equally enriching. I informed the doctors, especially the one designing the tool that I shall continue to disturb him and seek his guidance. He assured that he would send me some research work done on *Trigunas*.

Knowing that the concept of *Trigunas* was being researched upon in a formal laboratory reinforced my belief. I myself was aware of the changes that the nurturing of *Gunas* was having in my work life, family life and personal pursuits. I wondered, what heaven on earth meant!

Neha had come to pick me up at the station. In her state of inquisitiveness she suggested we go to our favourite café straightaway. She wanted minute-by-minute details of my trip and

Kumbh Mela

I could understand her plight. By now we were so deep into the concept of *Trigunas* that our daily lifestyle had been aligned and we could feel the change in our reactions and approach. However, sense prevailed and we drove back home to meet everybody first. We decided to go to the café the next day after an early dinner.

As we entered the café the next day I started telling her about my train journeys, to and fro, which were as enriching as the Kumbh *Mela* itself. I told her about the question that was popped at me by a stranger, the in-depth knowledge Vimal had about Amitabh Bachchan and the recent conversation with the group of doctors.

It was intriguing to know how ancient concepts were getting validated in laboratories. These research activities were in the true essence, working towards comprehending the truth rather than finding the truth in our comprehension as wisely stated by Kapil in the train. Now we were eager to know what research work had been undertaken in the field of *Gunas*. I called up the doctor to remind him to send me some research work. He assured me that he would send it to me by e-mail.

Neha told me that her patience had been pushed enough as she was waiting for me to come back so that we could continue our journey with Mr. Anonymous. She had not asked for the next set of papers from dad and was waiting for me to do so. So we went back home and the very next day we got our next bit of wisdom. Neha had already made a photocopy of the bunch before I came back from office. I was delighted to get home-cooked dinner after a gap of four days and we got back to our copies in hand.

Freedom from insecurities is any day preferred than having security, It's all in our mind.

CHAPTER FOURTEEN

MIND

Mind is not brain. Mind is not tangible. Mind is intelligence, Mind is non-intelligence, Mind is ego, Mind is modifications of the *Gunas*, as *Ayurveda* is to our physical body, *Trigunas* are to our mind. So it is important to know the composition of our mind.

The Mind has four facets to it:

1. *Manas*

2. *Buddhi*

3. *Chitta*

4. *Ahankaar*

1. *Manas*

Manas is the mind instrument which receives the signals from the outer world through the five windows of the body, i.e. ears, skin, eyes, tongue and nose. These five sense organs are our input vents. By itself, *Manas* is non-intelligent. *Manas* receives the signals from the sense organs and interprets the external world. These signals are then passed on to the other facets of the mind for further processing. After all the processing, the output signals are sent back to *Manas* for giving external reactions through the action organs, i.e. mouth, legs, hands, genitals and anus.

2. Buddhi

Buddhi is the intelligent facet of the mind. It is also referred to as the discriminating power, free will and intelligence in various compilations. *Buddhi* receives the cognition signals from the Manas and together with the other facets, *Ahankaar* and *Chitta*, it processes the thought and sends the signals back for action to the *Manas*. *Buddhi* plays the 'intelligence' part. A strong *Buddhi* may be able to connect the input signals to as much information stored in the mind (*Chitta* & *Ahankaar*) and give a well thought after output signal back to *Manas*. Even after connecting the input signals with the stored information, *Buddhi* has the intelligence to apply its own discriminating power before giving the output. *Buddhi* has the ability to make choices. It can also discriminate as to which information to store or negate.

3. Chitta

Chitta is where the memory and impressions are formed. It is the storehouse of the mind. *Chitta* is where personal likes and dislikes are stored. *Chitta* is also referred to as ego consciousness in various compilations. These impressions in *Chitta* are a potent form of action. In Sanskrit and Hindi these impressions are also known as *sanskaars*. *Sanskaars* are impressions formed in the *Chitta*, which look for a congenial external environment to convert themselves into actions. *Sanskaars* can be good or bad. A good, external environment will vent out good *sanskaars* while a bad external environment will vent out bad *sanskaars*. The behavioural pattern of the action is determined by the set of *Gunas*.

To help the aspirant visualise, *Chitta* is inherently not plane but has a surface with impressions of varying depths. The impressions are formed, deepened and filled on a daily basis. For example, whenever a person acts as per his likes or dislikes the respective impression in the *Chitta* is intensified. As a person becomes unattached to the feeling of like or dislike, the respective impression fades away. *Chitta* is full of preconceived notions that hamper clarity of thought.

The *Buddhi* is designed to take into account information and impressions from *Chitta* before giving output signals to *Manas* for action.

4. Ahankaar

Ahankaar is the basic feeling of 'I' that tends to govern all the actions of a human being. Statements like 'I like this' or 'I like that' find its origin in *Ahankaar*. If the *Buddhi* is weak the actions are governed by the preconceived impressions and the 'I'-ness of the person. If the *Buddhi* is strong, it can overcome the selfishness of *Ahankaar* and also the likes and dislikes stored in the *Chitta* to give a fair and just reaction to the outside world.

Most of us are often judgmental about others. This need to pass judgments is mainly to satisfy our *Ahankaar*.

After the mind processes the input signals, the output signals are sent to *Manas* which further puts the processed thought into action through *Karmendriyas* such as speech, leg movement, hand movement, reproduction, excretion, etc.

All four Facets put together form the perceptions and conceptions of a human being.

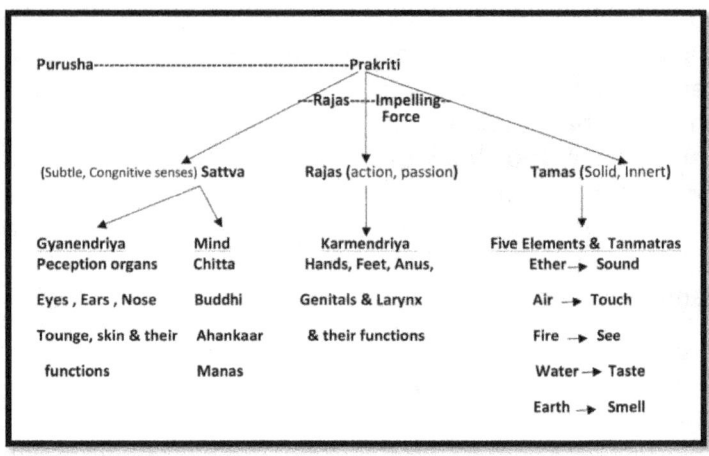

In India, when there was an outburst of AIDS there were many measures that were taken to control this disease. Amongst the measures, one of them was providing condoms on the highway to truck drivers. Travelling on long routes gave truck drivers an external environment and freedom to indulge in immoral activities. That does not mean all truck drivers indulge in prostitution, but the ones with such embedded impressions (*sanskaars*) in the mind got a congenial environment to vent out.

There is a thinking membrane that exists between the transformations of *sanskaars* to action. This membrane is *Buddhi* or free will or discriminating power that may be able to control the unleashing. Discriminating power is the capacity to execute choices. Even if a truck driver may have certain immoral *sanskaars* embedded in *Chitta* but a strong developed *Buddhi* may be able to execute a moral choice in accordance with its duties. If the *Buddhi* is made strong, it will first analyse the impression before reacting and thus vent a justified and unbiased action, thereby negating the impression of the *Chitta*.

Mind

Both of us were fascinated by the knowledge of the four facets of the mind. Neha could now explain her fear of dogs, she said "I had a dog bite when I was young and the incident seems to have left a long lasting impression on the *Chitta*. I do find the dogs in the neighborhood cute and my intellect (Buddhi) knows that I can touch them but is not strong enough to negate the impression in the *Chitta*." She continued "I will love to clean up my *Chitta* and make the intellect strong enough to take unbiased decisions."

"You seem to be in the right field for that," I remarked. We decided to get back to the facets of the mind as these were gifted moments by destiny.

Under the influence of *Rajas* the sensory organs are most active. Sensory organs send the signals from the external environment to the *Manas*. The Buddhi connects these signals received from *Manas* to the impressions in *Chitta* and *Ahankaar*. If the impressions in the *Chitta* are intense they tend to overrule the intelligence of the *Buddhi* and directly send the output signals to the *Manas*. The signals received from the sensory organs to *Manas* unite with the preconcieved impressions in the *Chitta* to vent out a response. This response is vented out in a certain behavioural pattern in accordance with the *Gunas*.

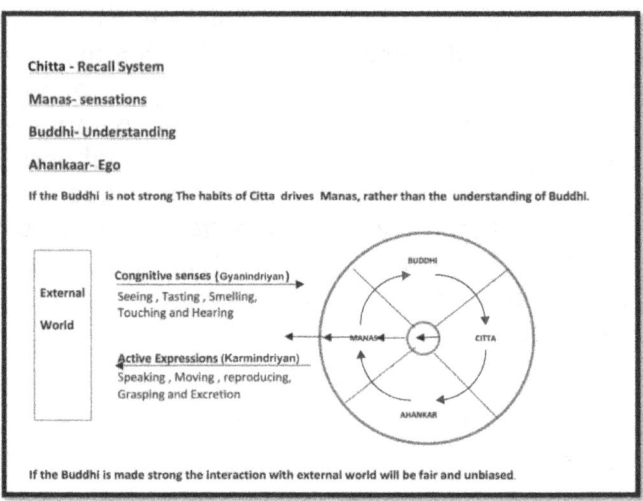

The *Upanishads* (*Kena Upanishad*) refers to '*Chitta Shuddhi*' or purifying the pre-conceived impressions as an important step. When the (*Chitta*) is purified and the mind has become pure, one attains self-knowledge and purity of thought, i.e. all actions thereon will be fair and just. The definition of Yoga as per Patanjali is '*Chitta Vritti Nirodh*'. Basically, cessation (*Nirodh*) of the modifications (*Vritti*) of the *Chitta* is Yoga.

In *Katha Upanishad* 1.3.5, a word of caution has been mentioned very aptly and it says, "If the intellect (*Buddhi*) is incapable of discriminating between right and wrong and the lower minds are uncontrolled, it is like a chariteer that has to deal with uncontrollable, vicious horses." Further, it is acknowledged, "He whose intellect '*Buddhi*' has control on the senses and mind '*Manas*', can realise his highest potential of human existence."

When a person evolves into *Sattva* he gets detached from the pairs of opposites: joy and sorrow, excitement and depression, pain and pleasure. Under this state of *Sattva* the *sanskaars* or pre-concieved impressions become weak and the discriminating power (*Buddhi*) starts to become strong. The actions of a pure *Sattvik* person further do not form any *sanskaars* or impressions in daily life because of his emotional detachment. *Buddhi* acts as an independent discriminating power, thus all actions are fair and not deluded by biases.

Awareness enhances discriminating power thereby releasing oneself from the bondages of *sanskaars*. Under the influence of *sanskaars* one may execute wrong actions despite the knowledge of it being wrong.

It is a rather disciplined path to tread and slips in this path are common. The *sanskaars* unconsciously transform into action. One way to control this unconscious transformation of *sanskaars* to action is by controlling the external environment one is exposed to. Avoid environments that may trigger and vent out unwanted *sanskaars* and thereby use that time to build one's discriminating power.

The basic attributes are common between an animal and a human being. Some of these commonalities are:

1. Humans eat, so do animals
2. Humans sleep, so do animals
3. Humans fear, so do animals
4. Humans procreate, so do animals

However, humans can analyse and think before reacting, while animals CANNOT.

So the basic difference between a human and an animal is the presence of *Buddhi*. This difference i.e. presence of *Buddhi*, is not apparent till the time this *Buddhi* is developed stronger by discipline. If the *Buddhi* is not developed, i.e. our reactions are an offshoot of our preconceived notions then there is not much of a difference between a human and an animal, apart from ourpotential to over power them.

"Mind has always been an interesting aspect, Mind power is limitless," said Neha.

I recollected having read extensively about Mind and its facets in *Upanishads*, and Patanjali Yog Sutras. An analogy between *Chitta* and a lake had been interesting and also a paradoxical approach between the eastern and western philosophy. I decided to share the analogy with Neha "*Chitta* is often visualised as a lake and *sanskaar* or impressions as the ripples in it. Multiple nonstop inputs from our sensory organs makes the lake turbulent. This turbulence reduces the effectiveness of the *Buddhi*. These ripples in the lake exist in all layers. The ripples in the lower layers inherently effect the ripples on the surface which we see as action in the lake. Some ripples in the lower layer of the lake die down and some get a vent on the surface manifesting into visible action. Neha, I can relate to this analogy so much more after reading this manuscript."

Neha agreed and prompted me to go on as she was completely engrossed in the analogy. Seeking the moment I elaborated on the paradoxical lens through which the eastern and the western philosophies look at the *Chitta*. "In the eastern philosophy all disciplines are designed to make the *Chitta* pure there by

Mind

aiming at freedom from the cycle of birth and death where as the western philosophy talks about how to use the *Chitta* to our advantage in this very life." I could sense Neha's thoughtful gaze. "The westerners relate the *Chitta* to the subconscious mind and indicate that this subconscious mind is where all the habits reside. Habits are actions that manifest subconsciously with least thought and effort, like nail biting or waking up time in the morning. Our breathing, heart beat etc. are all effortlessly managed by this subconscious mind or *Chitta*. So if we consciously introduce a positive habit in the subconscious mind, or as per analogy, consciously introduce a ripple in the lake it shall also manifest effortlessly in the real world."

Neha was surprised at the paradox and a minute of thoughtful silence followed. What came then was totally enlightening. Neha said, "There will be no use of introducing a ripple in a lake which is already turbulent. It is only after the lake is made calm that the desired effect of a consciously introduced ripple shall manifest." Neha continued to make the paradox into a seamless alignment. "A ripple can be introduced successfully only when the surface and the undercurrents are brought in control and then the ripple can be intensified into a wave if so desired." My face lit up , I added "I have observed many legendary batsmen in cricket hit the ball effortlessly. The batting techniques, after intense practice, get embedded in their subconscious mind and manifest effortlessly in their game. Neha, your insight has woven the eastern and the western philosophy into one seamless fabric." We smiled at each other and knew that this manuscript was stimulating the best in us.

An interesting incident came to my mind as I continued, "Last time we went to a water park with kids, my niece, Mansha, wanted to get on to a thrilling ride 'Torpedo', which had a vertical fall in the tube for 25 feet that led into a slide and then a pool of water. I accompanied her to the top, though I was feeling scared myself. Her chance came and she left it thrice for the next in line. I told her that if she backs off now she would not be able to enjoy such rides all her life. Not realising that after speaking those words of wisdom I would have to serve as an example too. Now there certainly was no chance left for me to miss my turn in the queue."

"After I took the plunge and went all the way down I climbed up the stairs again to fetch Mansha. I saw Mansha was still missing her turn with many others in the same state. I don't know what worked but she finally took the plunge and did not let an unnecessary impression of fear form on her *Chitta*. And I am sure my plunge also cleared my *Chitta* of unnecessary fear of heights. Recently she went on a school trip to the same water park, did the Torpedo with her friends and came back all excited. The incident suddenly seemed more insightful."

My plunge also puts light on another phenomenon. "If one acts as per the likes, dislikes or fear of the *Chitta*, he tends to make the impressions stronger and the intellect weaker. And so the old saying goes, 'The only way to overcome the fear is to face it'. It all seems so obvious now."

"The other facet, the 'I'-ness of ego (*Ahankaar*) also seems interesting," said Neha. "This 'I'-ness gives rise to the want of looking at oneself, in exclusivity to others. This exclusivity gives rise to the feeling of jealousy and greed."

Working to make our Buddhi strong suddenly seemed to be an important exercise. But we did not know about the gym or equipment that we needed to do so. Interestingly, dad told us the next set of papers was on just that.

Trigunas – The Ayurveda for Mind.

CHAPTER FIFTEEN

DISCIPLINES THAT MAKE BUDDHI STRONG

An Action is a thought that has been externalised. A thought is born in the Mind; it may be born due to an external influence or an internal influence or its cause may be a previous thought. At the time of the 'birth of a thought' the mind may be in a state of tranquility or aggressiveness. But the thought will have its own effect on the mind thereon. The pattern in which the thought is externalised into action depends on the set of *Gunas*.

After the thought is born it may or may not have a compatible impression on the *Chitta*. If it does not have any relevant impression on the *Chitta*, the *Buddhi* will work independently and take the thought to its logical conclusion, which may even be disposing it off completely. Whatever the *Budhhi* does with the thought it will not invoke any emotion. If the thought has a relevant impression on the *Chitta*, only then does it become an emotion. The intensity of the emotion depends upon the intensity of the impression on the *Chitta*. An emotion thus formed has the potential to disturb the mind and also energise the thought and action. An emotional outburst is due to this phenomenon. An emotion makes a thought fearless and courageous to drive it to a conclusive action.

Disciplines That Make Buddhi Strong

An emotion is a powerful thought and can have a positive or negative effect. An emotion nurtured after consultation with the discriminating power in its tranquil state can have a positive effect but this channelising of the emotions can only be done by a highly evolved mind. Usually, an emotion overrules the *Buddhi* and leads to delusion and disturbance. An emotion also drains a lot of energy and leaves a person in a tired state. There is a vast difference in the characteristics of a thought and an emotion. An emotion is like a flood and a thought is a stream. A thought can also be like a stagnant pool and lead to stagnation. If one can learn the art of channelising the emotion in the right direction as advised by the *Buddhi* one can get outstanding results. This can only happen in an evolved state of serenity and detachment. Attachment to the result or fruits can lead to intensifying of the emotion. In this state of attachment one usually overlooks consulting the *Buddhi*, leading to ill actions in a deluded state of mind.

An aspirant can only use the power of emotion positively by knowledge, awareness and tranquility. This state can only be achieved by complete detachment from the fruits of action. The action that originates through emotion has great force whereas an action that originates through the contemplative *Buddhi* is like a gentle stream. Emotion is a trait of *Rajas* and similar to *Rajas*, is a high-energy tool. This tool when used consciously by choice can get outstanding results.

Our mind is so designed that it has a checkpoint right before the finishing line. When any thought is on the verge of conclusion there always comes a point when a person tends to rethink whether he is doing the right thing or not. This last checkpoint is a blessing in disguise. There are many crimes that are avoided because of this checkpoint. There is also an irritation caused because of this last point of consultation with the *Buddhi* right before concluding one's action. This is a point where the *Buddhi* again has to take the right decision whether to conclude or not. But if the intensity of emotion is very strong then this last checkpoint is also overlooked.

Indecisiveness, delay, and the fear of making a decision because of this last check point can be painful. It is the *Buddhi* that is responsible for taking a timely decision. Some people live in a state of indecision for a long time because they are overtly cautious and are afraid to take a decision. Indecision beyond a point is worse than taking a wrong decision. In such a case the *Buddhi* needs to be made strong.

Such inaction or inertia is the outcome of the influence of *Tamas*. An action performed with a deluded state of mind is detrimental and is done under the influence of *Rajas-Tamas*, *Rajas* being predominant. *Rajas* is the *Guna* of action but *Tamas* deludes the mind resulting in ill action. Action taken under the state of tranquility and non-attachment is always the right action and can only be achieved under the influence of *Sattva*.

The ability to make a choice is strengthened by the discriminating power or the *Buddhi*. Therefore, to attain this ultimate state it is important to strengthen the *Buddhi*. There are two disciplines prescribed to make the Buddhi strong:

1. Meditation
2. Contemplation

1. Meditation

Meditation Or *Dhyana* is the sixth step in the 8 limbs of Patanjali's Yoga:

i. *Yam*
ii. *Niyam*
iii. *Aasana*
iv. *Pranyaam*
v. *Pratihaar*
vi. *Dhyaana*
vii. *Dharana*
viii. *Samadhi*

The subject of meditation has been widely written upon. It is so widely elaborated that it has become confusing. The goal is common in all the methods but the methods depicted are innumerable. For an aspirant to choose which method to adopt has become confusing. In this compilation we shall avoid enhancing the confusion by abstaining from recommendations.

With meditation one starts to acknowledge the presence of a serene 'inner space'. This inner space helps to detach oneself from the emotions of the circumstance thus analysing as a spectator. The goal of the eight limbs of Patanjali's Yoga as mentioned in *Patanjali Sutra* is '*Chitta Vritti Nirodh*'. *That* means, by following the Patanjali's method the *Chitta* of the mind shall become clear as a crystal. Thus all actions will be taken by the *Buddhi*, which will be unbiased and for the overall good of the society.

Meditation is not a solution to life's problems but is definitely a tool that prepares the mind to analyse and resolve the problems in life.

In the western world a new concept is gaining ground that is 'Mindfulness'. Mindfulness is concept of being aware of what is happening in the present – on a moment-to-moment basis. It is often noticed, even, in corporate meetings and conferences that the mind has a very limited span of attention. It often gets preoccupied with memories, future plans, worries, fantasies, etc. This loitering of the mind happens without awareness.

In the late 1970's there was an American instructor of Hath Yoga and Buddhist Meditation. His name was Jon Kabat-Zinn. He had been a student under the Buddhist meditation teachers and had also studied at the Insight Meditation Society in his early years. Mindfulness as a concept was introduced by him, which was the need of the hour in the corporate world. He designed training programmes that are now recognised by the University of Massachusetts. Mindfulness is also used as a tool for therapy for various stress-based diseases. It is a direct offshoot and a symptom of meditation.

The average attention span in 2000 was 12 seconds, which has now dropped to a single digit. Meditation not only increases one's attention span but also makes one aware of loss of attention. When one loses attention and is aware of the loitering of the mind one can make a conscious effort to resume his attention. Meditation is a practice to make the mind more aware, mindfulness thus enhances the skill to contemplate over long periods of time.

Being a student of Psychology and Yoga, I could see that Neha had a lot on her mind to share. She read out of the bunch, *'Emotion is a powerful thought and can have a positive or negative effect.'* This statement reminds me of the infamous Jessica Lal murder case that led to her getting shot in the head for refusing to serve a drink after closing hours of the bar. Anger and rage are very powerful negative emotions. Anger and rage

Disciplines That Make Buddhi Strong

in the shooter was so strong that it even broke through the last checkpoint of the mind and he pulled the trigger.

"On the other hand, the patriotic emotion of Mahatma Gandhi created such a wave that it had an effect across the length and breadth of the country. The emotion of one man was so strong that it got externalised into action across geographies. Under the civil disobedience movement and the salt march, large number of people were hit by the butt of the gun on their heads and they took the hit without a revolt."

"A thought may be peaceful or serene but when it gets influenced by an impression on the *Chitta*, it gets energised." Neha said, restating what Mr. Anonymous had written.

"Happiness can be derived from a serene and peaceful thought but when we use the word 'fun' it oozes some amount of energy, right!" Neha needed a nod to continue her insight, "Energy is an inseparable part of emotion, so if the emotion can be externalised in consultation with the *Buddhi*, it can be channelised positively."

"I always thought the people walking the path of serenity did not know what fun meant but it seems they have discovered their ways." I exclaimed.

Neha continued, "Being a Yoga student and instructor I always realised the importance of meditation but now it seems to be a precondition to have healthy fun."

I thought what Neha had just said made good sense and started to repeat the thought for more clarity, "Fun does have an aspect of emotion attached, it may lead to disastrous consequences but when the fun is in consultation with the *Buddhi* it becomes healthy fun."

Neha suggested we get back to the other discipline to make the *Buddhi* strong. i.e. contemplation. So we went on to read about the second discipline.

2. Contemplation

Contemplation is described in a very methodical manner in our scriptures. The four steps of contemplation are:

i. *Sravana*

The seeker gains knowledge of the source of wisdom. *Sravana* includes inputs by hearing, watching or reading. One must keep the company of like-minded people who can guide the seeker to various sources of wisdom. Nowadays, desperately looking for a guru for guidance can turn fatal.

ii. *Manana*

This includes understanding and questioning the logic of inputs until one is convinced. Delving on new concepts. Like a humming bee, one must collect fragrances from different flowers and convert them into honey.

iii. *Nididhyasana*

Assimilating the knowledge one has gained and living by it. In this step, the most important aspect is manifesting the knowledge into action. This is where 99% of aspirants may slip.

iv. *Sakshatkara*

Gaining knowledge in a wholesome way. This may include understanding higher realms of human existence that were unknown until now and revealing knowledge as the fountainhead of wisdom.

Contemplation refines the *Buddhi* in all aspects. A refined *Buddhi* acts on pure reason; action based on pure reason is unbiased and for the overall goodness of the society.

May it be nurturing of the *Gunas* or refining of the *Buddhi*, the most important step is to discipline oneself. A disciplined lifestyle leads to disciplined mind, action and speech. Such a lifestyle leads to clarity of thought and the mind is free of clutter. A Mind in this unchained state of freedom leads to phenomenal results and innovative thinking in personal and professional life.

Inevitably one tends to get stuck in a loop of thought. Thinking about the same subject or object leads to attachment to it. Attachment leads to infatuation. Infatuation leads to anger if it is not fulfilled, anger leads to delusion and destroys the mind. Getting stuck in a loop of thought is a common phenomenon. The loop can be broken by the analytical and discriminating power of the *Buddhi*, which is developed by meditation and contemplation. By consciously breaking away from this loop of thought one tends to put his mind to newer thoughts thereby increasing creativity and productivity.

Neha and I were in deep silence as we finished reading. Everybody has experienced emotions, thoughts, emotional outbursts and drain of energy thereafter but few must be aware of this kind of understanding. The process of consultation of *Buddhi* comes naturally to everyone but by becoming aware of the whole system one can increase productivity by making the right choices.

Neha finally broke the silence and remarked, "Just when I thought I had bagged most of the wisdom, there comes another enriching thought. Mr. Anonymous seems to have reached a state of *Samadhi*." She winked to gesture the pun.

She continued, "You know, I meet so many yoga aspirants practicing different kinds of meditation, the only difference being the point of focus in the initial levels. Some focus in the centre of eyebrows, some on the heart. Any which way, I think whatever works for the aspirant is fine. The essence is to learn to control one's thoughts and then focus it inwards to realise the self."

I took our conversation to the next topic – Contemplation. "Contemplation was an important aspect I had never thought of. The four steps of contemplation seem interesting. I totally agree with Mr. Anonymous that looking for a Guru desperately could prove disastrous in today's world." I could relate to an exposure I had recently had at the Kumbh. "At the Kumbh, once I had to wait for 30-45 minutes to cross a walk way. There was this three-four kilometer long procession with thousands of men carrying flags of the God-man arriving on an elephant. It was quite apparent that the procession was certainly not of devotees it was of men on daily wages, dressed in uniform. The pomp and show was to attract people to this self acclaimed godman who was making an arrival at the *Mela*. He was trying to woo devotees by his monetary power rather than his ability to be a fountainhead of knowledge.

"The first three steps of contemplation seem relevant in day to day living. The fourth step is an evolved state for a few. Seeking, questioning, delving, assimilating and implementing seem to be the main takeaways from the first three points. When the three points become a habit the fourth seems to be a natural progression." I was amazed at the in-depth wisdom of Mr. Anonymous.

I had an insight to share: "As I was meditating today after a gap of a week, I realised that the number of thoughts that were arising and subsiding in mind were far more than usual. And most of these thoughts were petty. There was no need to store them. It seemed that they were arising directly from the impressions of *Chitta* and disappearing thereafter. As mentioned by Mr. Anonymous, meditation is a tool to make the *Buddhi* strong. Making the *Buddhi* strong can also be done by making the impressions on the *Chitta* weak. I realised that when I meditate everyday these petty thoughts do not find storage in my *Chitta*, thus keeping it clean."

I have also noticed that people who meditate become more receptive to others. They are open to new perspectives. As meditation is a tool to reduce the impressions of the *Chitta*, it also reduces the emotional intensity in one's own beliefs, thus making the aspirant more receptive. The style of conversing of a person also becomes softer when it is not linked with an impression in the *Chitta*. Meditation may reduce the aggression in conversations but at the same time, one has the ability to use the same aggression in his dialect at will.

"The loop of thought as mentioned by Mr. Anonymous can become very irritating at times and requires a conscious effort to break." I recollected an incident, "Neha, you remember this one time a thought of buying a sofa-cum-bed came to my mind, which got suppressed after discussion in the family. In the meantime, I had checked out a few sofa-cum-beds on an e-commerce site. Since the thought did not go well with others in the family I consciously disposed it off my mind."

Neha nodded in acknowledgement.

"But to my surprise, these e-commerce guys had a skill of building a loop of thought in my mind. Every time I logged on the Internet, the photo of the sofa-cum-bed was displayed on every site I surfed, news or social networking. If one is not conscious of this formation of loop, he will check it out again and again till he pushes his family into buying it. This can get irritating for all, except the e-commerce company."

Neha smiled and remarked sarcastically, "Nice example, Mr. Wiseguy!"

The Concept of *Trigunas* and the Mind started constituting a part of our dinning table discussions. Dad even got the original Urdu bunch of papers spiral bound in order to preserve the invaluable words. The only problem was that he had sent the bunch to the shop through his granddaughter who got the binding done on the left side as usually done for English or Hindi scripts. Soon he gave us the next set of translated papers.

Meditation is not a solution to life's problems but is definitely a tool that prepares the mind to analyse and resolve the problems in life.

CHAPTER SIXTEEN

FREEDOM, CREATIVITY AND SATTVA

The universe, from the beginning, has had one constant phenomenon – a string of cause and effects. The creation started with a cause – the Big Bang – and the multiple effects thereafter became the multiple causes for the future. The same phenomenon holds good for every living being. We are also the product of cause and effect. The Hindu theory of *Karma* is all about cause and effect too. Every cause leads to an effect that in turn becomes the cause for the next effect. Every creation, every output, every result, every achievement is all about cause and effect.

Contemplating further on the phenomenon it can be easily demonstrated that if one becomes conscious of the intended effect, all that needs to be done is to make the cause happen. When the mind is focused on an intended effect, distractions do not have the space to nurture themselves. Our mind has the capacity to process only one thought at a time and that is why two thoughts at the same time leads to confusion. This cause and effect phenomenon can be broken down into smaller causes and smaller effects in the path of the intended effect.

Freedom, Creativity And Sattva

There is an old saying: "Success is 99% hard work and 1% luck." Hard work becomes a cause that leads to effect. In the Hindu philosophy of *Karma*, every cause has to have an effect. The effect of a cause may manifest in this birth or the next, but one thing is for sure and that is every cause will have an effect. So when the cause of a previous life has an effect in the present life, it is unexplainable and is called luck. Luck is cause and effect over different births. I do not intend to introduce the concept of rebirth in this compilation. The intention of mentioning the concept is just to explain that our present causes are definite to have effects so one should be thoughtful of one's actions.

There are two kinds of cause. One is the instrumental cause and the second is the material cause. Like the clay is the material cause of the pot and the potter is the instrumental cause of the same pot. The same pot when completed can be appreciated in two aspects: one is the clay or material used and the other is the contribution the potter gave to the pot i.e. his mind or creativity. This creativity of the potter that has gone into making of the pot, will remain a part of the pot till its existence.

Likewise, our existence can also be acknowledged in two aspects: one is the gross body, which is our outer covering or material cause. The other is our subtle body, which consists of our mind (*Manas, Buddhi, Chitta, Ahankaar*), breath, five organs of action and five organs of knowledge. So when we become an instrument to any cause or creation we lend our gross body in terms of physical action and our subtle body in terms of intellect or 'creativity'. The potter in the process of creating a pot gives it a part of his subtle body in terms of an aura of the pot.

Creativity comes from freedom. And freedom is a state of mind. It is freedom or detachment from the fruits of the action. The action itself never creates bondage in the mind; it is the attachment or repeated thought of the outcome of action that causes the bondages and kills the freedom. The outcome should be given a thought but only for reviewing the path of action. Getting lured towards the outcome kills the freedom in the path of action. The moment this very potter gets attached and lured towards the monetary benefit that his pot is going to fetch him it will kill his freedom and thus his creativity.

I have observed good artists getting attached to the monetary benefits that their paintings fetch, thereby losing creativity that their work carried earlier. His freedom to create becomes limited because of his attachment to the benefits. He will make, but not create.

Freedom or detachment enhances creativity and intellectual contribution to whatever one does. Freedom is a state of mind and can be enjoyed in all kinds of preoccupation. Freedom is actually not from work but freedom from attachment to fruits of work. To reiterate this point, 'attachment to the effect in the cause-effect theory creates bondages and limits the creativity'.

As mentioned earlier, the element of freedom increases as one evolves from *Tamas* to *Rajas* to *Sattva*. *Sattva* is the state of mind that is detached from the outcome or fruits of action and therefore has least bondages. A *Sattvik* mind is a free mind. It exudes creativity and contributes highly in terms of intellect.

As we finished our reading, Neha exclaimed, "Wow, that was some thought!" The exclamation was followed by minutes of silence. After that she continued, "It seems to be a continuous string of thoughts. I wonder how Mr. Anonymous is able to evolve one thought for so long and nurture it to this level of understanding. He must be meditating regularly!" concluded the Yoga expert.

"He has built an organisation from scratch, which itself is an everlasting creation. He has lent his creativity and intellect to his organisation and wants to pass the mantra of cause and effect to his team," I reiterated. "I recently read about another such personality who lent his creativity to New Delhi by giving it the Metro Train. He actually gave a copy of *Gita Makaranda* to any new management personnel who joined his team."

"Mr. Sreedharan was the Managing Director and Chairman of the Delhi Metro project. He was awarded the Padma Shri award in 2002 and Padma Vibhushan in 2008 by the Indian government. The French government also gave him the highest civilian award i.e. the Chevalier de la Legion d'Honneur (Knight of the Legion of Honour). *TIME* Magazine gave him the title 'Asia's Heroes'." I got up to get the reference book that had his interview.

Neha gave a smile and said, "A legendary personality from Delhi, a propagator of the Concept of *Triguna*, a man living a life aligned with the lifestyle mentioned in the Gita... He, Mr. Sreedharan, just might be our Mr. Anonymous!"

Mr. Sreedharan is a projects man and is famous for completing the Konkan railways project and the Delhi Metro project. The Konkan Railway project is in the hilly area of the Western Ghats. He was made the Managing Director and Chairman of the project after his retirement from the Indian Railways in 1990. The Konkan Railway cover 760 kilometers with 93 tunnels and 150 bridges and was completed in record time. It is a feather in the cap of Indian Railways, which is the largest network of railways in the world. Thereafter at 65, he was made the Chairman of the challenging Delhi Metro project, which again he completed successfully in the specified time and budget. Now he is retired and leads a simple life in his village in Kerala.

I started reading out of the magazine, "'*To foster values, a copy of* Gita Makaranda *is given to all employees when they join.* "I do not consider it a religious text. It is an administrative gospel that teaches you how to face challenges and overcome them," *says Mr. Sreedharan. T*he main essence of Gita Makaranda is detachment from fruits of duty and it has chapters dedicated to the concept of *Trigunas*.'"

On reading further we were amazed to observe how he had disciplined his life to nurture *Sattva*. He gets up at 4:30 am and concludes his morning with Yoga and meditation. He is punctual to office and back home. He retires to bed by 10 pm and again starts at daybreak. His *Aahaar* is also designed to nurture *Sattva Guna*. After studying in detail his lifestyle, accomplishments and acknowledging his knowledge of *Trigunas* we were convinced that legends are a result of conscious nurturing and not a stroke of luck.

We finally got our hands on the last set of papers that we had given to dad. I got reminded that these were not the last set of papers that I had found. I had kept the first paper and the last couple of papers in my wardrobe to avoid questions about the identity of Mr. Anonymous.

By now I had enough reverence for Mr. Anonymous to accept him as my mentor even without meeting him. His thoughts were so alive in the papers that he had written. I just hoped that he is still alive and I am able to take his blessing in person.

Neha and myself took the last set of papers given by dad and huddled in our cozy corner to have another spurt of enriching moments.

Different paths same result

In the Bhagavad Gita Chapter 13, Verse 24, 25 and 26, Shri Krishna prescribes four paths that an aspirant can follow in his life to realise the higher potential of human existence.

One of them is by practicing Yoga, i.e. by treading the path of 8 limbs of Ashtang Yoga, namely *Yama, Niyama, Aasana, Pyanayama, Pratyahara, Dharana, Dhyana* and *Samadhi*. *Yama* and *Niyama* are the ethical preparations without which one cannot evolve; nonviolence, truthfulness, cleanliness, austerity and so forth. *Aasana* prepares the physical body to reach a level of fitness so that the body can remain still, it does not distract the mind with any signal of discomfort when practicing further. *Pranayama*, prepares the breath and internal movements of the body, like that of the lungs, not to distract the mind when engaged in the next step. Thereafter the aspirant learns to withdraw his senses (*Pratyahara*) and then to focus his mind (*Dharana*). Single point focus leads to Meditation (*dhyana*) and prolonged steady meditation leads to *Samadhi*.

The second path that is prescribed in the Gita to elevate to higher planes is the path of Knowledge. On this path, the aspirant gains the knowledge of Scriptures – i.e. *Vedas, Upanishads, Brahma Sutras* and Gita. He contemplates on the same and aligns his life to the wisdom thus gained. With thorough understanding and contemplation the aspirant's mind becomes discriminative of the path he decides to follow. His mind becomes uncluttered and does not get distracted easily by inherent materialistic desires.

An aspirant who does not have the inclination to read through the scriptures, becomes a follower of a Sage/Seer. He implements the knowledge imparted by the Sage with full devotion and faith to reach higher spiritual planes. The wrong choice of Sage or Guru can lead to disastrous consequences.

Majority of us live in the real world of duties, society pressures and inherent desires. We do not have the inclination to go through Yoga (beyond the fitness aspect of it), scriptures or follow a Sage/Guru.

For most of us, there is a prescribed path that aligns with our fulfilment of worldly duties. This path can be tread to avoid sufferings and frustrations, thereby making life a delightful experience in this very real world.

The four basic mantras of treading this path are:

1. Performing our duty skillfully.
2. Not getting attached to the fruits (outcome) of actions (duty) thus performed.
3. Egoless Living.
4. '*Sambhav*' – To refrain from excitement or depression, thus maintaining a state of calmness and serenity.

The four points mentioned above are easier said, than done. The life with above-mentioned attributes is actually a delight to live. The paradigm shift required to follow the attributes mentioned can be done by nurturing the *Gunas* in a predetermined proportions.

We took a minute to appreciate the overall completeness of the compilation written by Mr. Anonymous. We realised that he has taken time to even write about the cautions that a reader must take while treading the path of *Trigunas*. The next heading was 'Word Of Caution'.

Mr. Sreedharan's lifestyle, accomplishments and knowledge of Trigunas convinced us that legends are a result of conscious self nurturing and not a stroke of luck.

CHAPTER SEVENTEEN

WORD OF CAUTION

Word Of Caution

In the ancient scriptures there is a story of Narasimha, a reincarnate of Lord Vishnu that serves as a word of caution for aspirants. Knowledge, although teaches the aspirant to be humble and compassionate but ironically it also tends to feed the Ego.

Once there was a very learned person named Hiranyakashyap. He undertook many years of penance and austerity in devotion to Lord Brahma. After attaining Lord Brahma's attention, he asks the Lord for a boon of immortality. Lord Brahma declined the request of immortality but offers to bind the event of death of Hiranyakashyap to near impossible conditions. Thus Hiranyakashyap asks, 'O my lord, the giver of blessings, if you will kindly grant me the blessing I desire, please let me not meet death from any of the living entities created by you. Grant me that I not die within any residence or outside any residence, during the daytime or at night, nor on the ground or in the sky. Grant me that my death not be brought about by any weapon, nor by any human being or animal..."

As agreed Lord Brahma binds Hiranyakashyap's death to such impossible conditions so that he may never die. During a violent situation, Kayadu the wife of Hiranyakashyap is saved by a divine sage called

Narad. Under the protection of Narad the unborn child of Hiranyakashyap in the womb of his wife Kayadu is influenced by the devotional qualities of the sage Narad. The child, Prahalaada, gets sage-like qualities and becomes a devotee of Lord Vishnu.

Once, when Prahalaad is involved in the rituals of submission to Lord Vishnu, his father, Hiranyakashyap insists on his supremacy over Lord Vishnu. When asked, Prahlaada refuses to acknowledge his father as the supreme lord of the universe and claims that Vishnu is all-pervading.

Hiranyakashyap points to a nearby pillar and asks if 'his Vishnu' is in it and says to his son, "Prahlaad, O most unfortunate, Prahlaad, you have always described a supreme being other than me, a supreme being who is above everything, who is the controller of everyone, and who is all-pervading. But where is He? If He is everywhere, then why is He not present before me in this pillar?'

Prahlaada then answers, 'He is in pillars, and He is in the smallest twig.'

Hiranyakashyap, unable to control his anger, smashes the pillar and attacks Prahlaada, following the sound, Vishnu appears in the form of Narasimha and moves to attack Hiranyakashyap in defence of Prahlaada. In order to kill Hiranyakashyap and not upset the boon given by Brahma, the form of Narasimha is chosen. Hiranyakashyap can not be killed by human, *deva* or animal. Narasimha is neither one of these as he is a form of Vishnu incarnate as a part-human, part-animal. He comes upon Hiranyakashyap at twilight (when it is neither day nor night) on the threshold of a courtyard (neither indoors nor out), and puts Hiranyakashyap on his thighs (neither earth nor space). Using his

Word Of Caution

sharp fingernails as weapon, he kills the arrogant Hiranyakashyap.

This story should act as a word of caution to all aspirants of the *Triguna* concept. With a disciplined life one tends to feel self-righteous. Self-righteousness often manifests as disrespect of people following other paths of wisdom. It is important for an aspirant to acknowledge and respect all sources of wisdom. The path should make a person humble and compassionate rather than arrogant and self-righteous.

A smile of disgust came to Neha's face as she finished reading the 'word of caution'. She said, "The arrogance and self-righteousness is very evident in many god-men in the society." I could sense an emotion in her thought as she continued. "Often these god-men have crossed the line of dignity with women. They might have started on the right path but as people fall to their feet thereby feeding their ego, they think they can get away with anything." I could make out that she was referring to the recent case of molestation by Asaram Bapu, an infamous god-man who went to jail thereafter.

After a moment of silence I shared my thought, "Over the years as I have assimilated knowledge from the scriptures, I have voluntarily disciplined my self and withdrawn from habits and objects of sensory pleasures. As mentioned in the scriptures, slowly the aspirant gets relieved of the pull of the sense pleasures. In this transformation the aspirant is often exposed and challenged by the vibes of the pleasure objects and habits but his *Buddhi* should be evolved to a level where he can contemplate, introspect and make a determined choice to avoid such habits and objects. More often than not, the *Buddhi* of the aspirant has not evolved enough to that level and he tends to slip back into pleasure seeking habits." I believed strongly in what I was saying, as I have experienced the pull and the slip towards old habits and lifestyle. "As the aspirant is treading his path and making his *Buddhi* strong the devotees fall to his feet thereby feeding his ego and giving him a Guru status. Although the aspirant has not reached the Guru level, he is elevated by the reverence of the devotees desperately looking for a Guru. The bloated ego deludes his mind with a sense of status and power. The ego feed and the 'pleasure-seeking trait' strengthens the *Rajas* and makes it dominate the *Sattva*. Slowly, the ego is continued to be fed by the ever-growing number of devotees and the *Sattva* gets overshadowed by *Tamas*. Under the influence of *Rajas* and *Tamas*, the deluded mind nurtures extreme pleasure-seeking thoughts that are externalised into ill actions."

"The word of caution is very relevant to every aspirant in the path of action or knowledge," Neha emphasised. "The ego and self-righteousness should be kept under control by an aspirant following the path of knowledge or action because he is the doer in both the paths. In the path of devotion the chances of slipping are less as the aspirant submits himself to god and is not the doer of action or assimilator of knowledge in this path."

"This word of caution is important for all disciplined men and not only for god-men. When a person is the doer of disciplined actions he is likely to achieve the desired fruits that may feed his ego and self-righteousness. So the word of caution is important for every person who is consciously gaining knowledge and doing the right action."

We got back to reading. The next few pages seemed to be about day to day discipline.

Moksha - Removing the I-ness

Most of our scriptures are aligned to the goal of *Moksha*. The meaning of *Moksha* is two fold. One is psychological and the other philosophical. Psychologically *Moksha* is removing the I-ness in a person, i.e *Moksha* can be attained by nurturing the right set of *Gunas*. It is liberation from attachment to self. Philosophically *Moksha* is freedom from the cycle of birth and death. Psychology is a stream of science and thus more acceptable to the present generation. We now live in a world dominated by science and technology.

The basis of science is validation and proof, whereas the basis of spirituality is faith and belief. According to science we need to first prove and validate before believing. According to spirituality we need to have belief and faith – the validation can happen over a period of time. This difference in the very basis of science and spirituality is evident in the time difference of acceptability of various phenomenon in the two fields. Spirituality accepted the cognition over space and time much before science came out with the theory of telepathy. Spirituality supported the theory of birth-death and rebirth, modern psychology now believes in past life regression as a means of therapy. Science waited for Newton to prove gravity and Archimedes to prove buoyancy before accepting gravity and buoyancy as phenomena.

Nowadays our paradigm has shifted towards science, we only believe in what has been proven and validated. The philosophical meaning of *Moksha* seems ambiguous to the present generation. Psychologically, *Moksha* means the removal of I-ness in a person. I-ness is the attachment of a person to self and a reason for delusion. Thus liberation from the attachment of self leads to clarity and fairness in action, it also does away with the biggest fear; the fear of death.

The philosophical goal is not yet proven by science and has become a deterrent for us to pick up and read our scriptures. We are forgetting that most part of our scriptures mainly talk about living a better quality of life here and now. I have read a lot of scriptures and feel that the psychological goal of removal of I-ness in a person paves way to live a good quality of life. By good quality of life I mean a life with happiness, health, clarity of thought and above average performance of duty.

To this context I remember Shri Aurobindo's words "When I turn my look towards the earth, I see that man's field of action, however large it may be, is terribly restricted. A man, who, in his mind and even in his vital being is vast like the universe, or atleast like the earth, as soon as he begins to act, is shut up within the narrow limits of material action, very bounded in its field and results."

Dincharya

Shri Krishna acknowledges in the Gita that despite the brutalities and massacres of the war, Mahabharatha was the need of the society. Mahabharatha led to the destruction of all the kingdoms, which thereafter came under one governance; it was an act of rectification of the society. The kings were getting involved in excessive pleasure seeking activities at the cost of governance. They were busy appreciating dance, music and sensuality. A king's duty is to give good governance towards the society. Their overindulgence in pleasure and neglect of duty led to the painful downfall and death of millions. The pleasure seeking habits had reached such heights that rectification without destruction was not possible.

Contrary to the general perception, our scriptures are very practical. They not only define the ideal but also prescribe how the self can be aligned to the ideal. I say this not only from knowledge but also after substantial implementation. An initial effort to align eating habits, thoughts, routine and recreation is definitely required. Thereafter the mind is more discriminative of thoughts and is in a state of calmness. The ego optimises to levels where life is free of negativity and hassles. A mind with clarity of thought becomes exponentially productive. One might miss the feeling of being overtly excited but at the same time is relieved of the feeling of sadness and depression. Less time and energy is wasted in these emotions giving more time to be positively engaged.

The initial alignment of lifestyle to nurture the predetermined *Gunas* does require some conscious effort. These initial, conscious efforts can be comfortably included in '*Dincharya*' or daily routine. A consciously imbibed *Dincharya* is the key to nurturing of the *Gunas*. A *Dincharya* that helps in predominance of the *Sattva Guna* is elaborated repeatedly in our scriptures. It is mentioned in the various *Smritis* like the *Yajnavalkya Smriti* and *Narada Smriti* and also finds mention in *Mahabhasya* of the Patanjali. It is most popularly elaborated in the *Manu Smriti* with 2685 verses. *Dincharya* is a important topic in the ancient texts of Yoga and *Ayurveda*.

It is inherent for our senses to go astray. Sense organs are like fire, the more we feed them with pleasures the more they go out of control. Sense organs cannot be tamed by non-indulgence; they can be tamed by knowledge and by following a consciously determined *Dincharya*. *Dincharya* or a daily routine is the basis of nurturing *Gunas*. Dominance of a particular *Guna* manifests into a desired character and personality.

These austerities and *Dincharya* are written in accordance with the lifestyle followed thousands of years ago. The circumstances of an aspirant in 3000 BC were certainly very different than the circumstances of a present aspirant of 2000 AD, although humanity and the Concept of *Trigunas* is the same. The nurturing methods follow the same basics, only the initial efforts (*Dincharya*) need to be aligned to present circumstances.

Word Of Caution

Sr. no.	Ancient Dincharya	Remarks	Suggested Present alignment
1.	A healthy person should wake up 1 hour before sunrise. i.e. approx. 5 am. This is the time with maximum *Sattva* in the air.	(Dincharya) exceptions – very young and old, Parents of infants and people not keeping well, etc.	Can be done in present times also. Waking up early does not mean sleeping less. It can only be achieved by sleeping by 9-10 pm.
2.	Should drink 750 ml to a litre of water stored in copper container in the morning.	(Dincharya)	Can be followed even today.
3.	One should wash their face with water at normal temperature. Brushing of teeth should be done for minimum 2 minutes. While splashing eyes with water one should fill the mouth with water. Do *Jal Niti* periodically.	(Dincharya)	Can be followed even today.
4.	Traditionally, inhalation of herbal smoke every morning is recommended.		Can be forgone

Sr. no.	Ancient Dincharya	Remarks	Suggested Present alignment
5.	One should excrete facing north in the morning and south in the evening. During excretion one should remain quiet	(Dincharya)	Was easily possible in ancient times but now changing direction is not possible.
6.	A five-minute self oil massage should be done on the scalp, limbs and more importantly under the feet. And a drop of oil in the nose.	(Dincharya)	Can be followed even today.
7.	Physical exercise to one fourth or one half of one's capacity is recommended. Followed by breathing exercises.	(Dincharya)	Can be followed even today.
8.	Bathing now will remove excess oil and clean the body.	(Dincharya)	Can be followed even today.
9.	Spend 15 minutes to 30 minutes of reading from a source of wisdom (Gita, Quran, etc.) Then meditate for a few minutes to an hour. This is most important to nurture the *Sattva Gunas* via *Vichaar* (thoughts).	(Dincharya)	Can be followed even today.

Word Of Caution

Sr. no.	Ancient Dincharya	Remarks	Suggested Present alignment
10.	A wholesome nourishing breakfast in a happy state of mind. Do not be critical of the food and avoid any kind of anger on the dining table.	Hereafter one is ready to deliver outstanding performance in one's occupation and need not devote any more time on self.	
11.	Lunch at 1 pm and dinner between 7-8 pm. Both meals should be followed by 10-minute walk to aid digestion.		
12.	Align eating habits (*Aahaar*) to *Sattva* as much as possible. Try and keep a fast once a week. Daytime fruit diet followed by a proper dinner.	This will help practice self-restraint which in-turn builds will power.	
13.	Recreation (*Vihaar*) – Listen to peaceful, soothing music that enhances serenity		
14.	Thoughts (*Vichaar*) – Avoid negative and emotional conversations. Learn to control one's thoughts and curb a negative thought as it arises.		

Sr. no.	Ancient Dincharya	Remarks	Suggested Present alignment
15.	Routine (*Achaar*) – Follow a predefined daily routine and avoid deviation.	Avoiding deviation will require initial effort but one will soon realise that the effort is worth the result.	

Over a period of time, our reading was having an effect on us and we started avoiding tea/coffee and discovered a whole new set of non-stimulant beverages to assist us in our conversations. Neha had bought a set of glass kettle and cups, which could brew as much natural tea as desired in a sitting by just pouring boiling water in it. It was soothing to taste the different flavours of fresh leaves. She would fill the perforated capsule of the kettle with fresh leaves of lemon grass or mint. Concoctions with freshly grated ginger and honey became more interesting. Tea for us meant brewed natural flavor in hot water rather than the mandatory use of tealeaves. And we could sit for hours sipping and delving over thoughts.

Neha started with her academic inputs on *Dincharya*. "There are broadly two *Samhitas* that give us the knowledge of *Ayurveda* – one is the *Sushrut Samhita* and the other is the *Charak Samhita*. The *Sushrut Samhita* is about surgery and the *Charak Samhita* talks about medicine with chapters dedicated to *Dincharya*. A consciously designed *Dincharya* prevents a person from all kinds of misery."

I quipped, "Misery! It seems waking up at 5 am actually takes away one's financial misery as well. The CEO of Apple, Tim Cook; CEO of Walt Disney, Robert Iger; CEO of Xerox and PepsiCo, Ursula Burns and Indra Nooyi respectively, all wake up at 5 am including the founder of Virgin group Richard Branson."

"It's no joke," Neha clarified, "According to our scriptures early morning hours are called *Brahma Mahurat*. Waking up at this time does take away all your miseries and assist in improving productivity. This includes taking away one's financial misery as well. The *Brahma Mahurat* has all the *Sattvik* qualities. These hours are more balanced and harmonious rather than active (*Rajas*) or inert (*Tamas*). The mind is fresh; nature comes alive with the sunrise. As the outside so the inside; the purity on the outside reflects in purity of our thoughts. This is the best time of the day for meditation. According to our scriptures, the *Brahma Mahurat* begins 1 hour 30 minutes before sunrise i.e. anytime from 4 am to 6 am is *Brahma Mahurat*."

"I like that 'As the outside so the inside'," I added. "After all, everything inside is the replica of everything outside. The biggest unit, the Universe, with its sun, planets, orbits is actually so similar to the smallest unit, the atom, with its nucleus and electron. Everything seems to be in a 24-hour cycle – the sun, planets, plants, animals, humans, etc. This 24-hour cycle also defines bigger cycles like the seasonal cycles of the years and even bigger cycles thereon. It is only when our lifestyle is in harmony with the entire ecosystem that we can bring out the best in ourselves. We are just a micro unit of the macro existence. The *Brahma Mahurat* gives us an opportunity to breath in and assimilate the harmonious *Sattvik* qualities to take on the day with serenity."

"I need to add a word of caution here," I continued, "The word harmony means 'pleasing combination'. The act of waking up in the morning has to be a pleasing act. The habit might require initial effort to inculcate but finally it has to be a pleasing habit to continue. The habit of waking up in the *Brahma Mahurat* has to be combined with the habit of sleeping by 10:00 pm

The CEO and MD of SAP for Indian subcontinent died due to a heart attack at the age of 42 years. Mr. Ranjan Das had run the Chennai Marathon a couple of months before his death; he was the youngest CEO of a multinational company in India. A few days before the fateful day he had confessed in an interview with NDTV of getting less sleep. He believed that four hours of sleep was enough, according to a source who was interviewed by the *Times of India*."

"People make an effort of waking up early," Neha opined, "Rather it is more important to make an effort to sleep on time. One has to get his seven to eight hours of sleep to remain healthy. The sleep hours can decrease with increase of fitness levels but scientifically, less than six hours is harmful for the body."

"All nurturing can start with *Dincharya*," I concluded.

One who knows when to stop, falls into no danger.

CHAPTER EIGHTEEN

PARTING WORDS

I dug into my wardrobe to find the three urdu papers I had kept safely. The top paper seemed to be an introductory script and the last two were beyond my grasp. I gave the papers to Dad and requested him to decipher them too. I told him, "These were papers from the same bunch that did not pertain to the main essence of the subject. Now after reading the wisdom of Mr. Anonymous we are intrigued to meet him in person. His writings had guided us to a better lifestyle; we owe him a visit to take his blessings."

Looking at the aged papers Dad expressed hesitantly, "It has been an insightful journey for me too. It has been evolving! My thought process and habits have sought more meaning. My sleep has become more blissful and my days have become more productive.

The whole concept makes sense but are you sure he will be alive? This bunch seems to have been written years back. It is most likely that his date of birth must be before 1947, because that is when Urdu was taught in schools of undivided India."

"If he is alive it shall be our greatest fortune to meet him. Although he has penned down his wisdom for a set of people in his company, me finding the bunch after a decade or more

Parting Words

might be a lead," I stated. Sensing the intensity in our pursuit, dad assured us the translated script by the weekend.

In the mean time, I received a few research papers[1] from the doctors in Bangalore. I was amazed to see how extensively the Concept of *Trigunas* had been researched over the years. Every research has to document all the previous research work done on the subject in a tabulated form to make sure it is not repeated. Reading through the research papers was interesting and tedious. I photocopied a few pages to discuss with Neha the next time we sit at our cozy corner. These discussions had really worked for us. Somehow, I wanted to continue to steal that time with Neha. It rekindled a one on one connect that was otherwise fading away as we grew from two to four in our family.

The fact that the Concept of *Trigunas* had been validated in laboratories and further tools had been developed to measure a set of *Gunas* in a person left us awestruck. I earnestly wanted to meet Mr. Anonymous and I hoped he was still alive. He must be a person who has lived a life in adherence to the concept in the present circumstances. His company would serve as case study on the effect of *Gunas* in the corporate world. An organisation led by a leader with the philosophy. His interpersonal family relationships could bring out what the *Gunas* can make of a person as a human being. I personally had started treading the path of living by the *Gunas*. It would be interesting to know the character and persona that time shall carve of me. Mr. Anonymous might serve as a living example.

I requested dad to translate and give me as much information about Mr. Anonymous as possible. He himself

---

[1] Research paper extracts can be found in the appendix.

was hoping to meet him one day and shower his reverence. So finally he gave me the translation of the first and the last two pages. Neha and I started reading the translation with hope of meeting Mr. Anonymous.

Namaskar,

It has indeed been a pleasure to build this organisation. Some of you have been with this organisation since 1967. The team has grown over the past four decades to over 12,000 across three continents. This growth has only been possible because of our belief – the only constant is change. We come from the age when phone calls to a different city had to be booked and awaited. We have been instrumental in changing the field of communication and bringing humanity closer.

I have often been called 'paradox personified'. I admit to the allegation. I have led an organisation which has constantly reinvented itself; we have moved with the times and are known for our creative thinking and innovative products. We have moved from a B2B industry to a B2C. Now we connect millions of hearts across India and other continents. I must thank my team who have lived with this paradoxical leader for more than 40 years.

I am told about my paradoxical attribute of leading the most dynamic company in the industry and yet clinging to my philosophies – shelving profit-making products to use the same assembly line for path breaking new technology and yet living by my age old beliefs. I admit to living a life by my philosophies. Let me also acknowledge, I am what I am because of these beliefs. These beliefs have given me the freedom to be creative; rather they have taught me that freedom is creativity. We have always taken decisions free from the lures of its

Parting Words

fruits. Every decision has always led us further towards freedom. We have always done what's best for the team and the industry.

I know other companies have often tried to lure our Chief Technical Officer and Chief Executive Officer with more lucrative offers. But we have been together for over half a century. This togetherness has only survived because of the belief in our philosophy. We were in college when we delved into the depths of our scriptures, our discussions often led to implementation. Together we lived every belief, experienced every symptom, the rest just happened. We, as senior management have never tried to impose our beliefs on our fellow team members. Now the time has come that we want to share our *Mantra* and leave the rest to thee.

Best Wishes!

Thank You Note

We have come a long way, I being the eldest of three, have been revered by my two cousin brothers. I cannot appreciate enough the support that I have got from them. We have held together through thick and thin, we have built on each other's strengths. Our endeavour has been to complement each other's attributes rather than trying to overshadow. We thank our fathers who have taught us the art of making heaven on earth.

Dutiful men never retire, they merely change their roles. I shall always be with the rest of you and shall continue to give time to our creation. I wish the entire team all the best and may you find the Concept of *Trigunas* good enough to live by. Request you to erase my name from every nook and corner as it may feed my ego. I intend to live in the present and make it worth my while, wherever I am. Let me not live in the past glories and abscond myself to service my present.

Please feel free to visit me at my home or in office for any service that you need of me.

Goodbye!

P.S.: Vijender Pahwa – I have tried to pour as much as it seemed relevant. Even if 5% of readers are able to assimilate and implement, I will think I have done my bit.

"Finally, a name!" Neha exclaimed. As we read the last of the translation we knew that we were meant to find Mr. Anonymous. There seemed to be enough information on him. He was certainly in the communication industry. His brothers were probably still active in the organisation. By all calculations he would be over 65 years when he wrote this piece around 2007, four decades from 1967. That means he must be in his mid-seventies now. He must have taken long to write this piece and the fact that I found it in central Delhi means he was in the National Capital Region. His organisation has done some path breaking work in its industry. Assembly line means some kind of a tangible product.

I immediately grabbed my laptop to look for Mr. Vijender Pahwa on the internet. I was sure we would find Mr. Anonymous soon. "Telecommunication, B2C, connecting hearts of a million, head office in NCR, and finally a name."

Parting Words

I was already looking forward to meeting Mr. Anonymous within a week. Neha exclaimed, "He must be in his seventies, a satisfied man. I wonder how his family would have carved out to be. He must be an aggressive personality or a docile personality. Let's visit his home together this week."

Meanwhile I had 17 Vijender Pahwas to filter through. LinkedIn came to our rescue. I started filtering aloud, "Vijender Pahwa Ford, no, Vijender Pahwa News Corp, no, Vijender Pahwa Simbi Mobile solutions, may be, Vijender Pahwa Taj Hotels, no, Vijender Pahwa Airmax India, maybe, Vijender Pahwa Orient IT, no… now we have two prospects Simbi Mobile Solutions and Airmax India."

Airmax India was the biggest mobile instrument manufacturer in India, it was B2C, and now exported all over the world. Neha pitched in, "Simbi solutions seems to be B2B whereas Airmax of course is B2C but too big to enter."

"The head office of Airmax is the huge glass building in Gurgaon," I pointed out to which Neha added, "We might not be able to pass through its security gates, let alone meet Mr. Vijender Pahwa."

"Neha, I have been in sales long enough to do that. We have a name and it's good enough to get through," I said.

I took an off on Monday. We dressed in formal attire and by 11 am we were at the reception of Airmax India asking for Mr. Vijender Pahwa. The receptionist politely asked us if we had an appointment to which I tactfully replied that we intended to speak to him on the intercom and not meet him. She looked at us suspiciously and asked for our visiting cards.

My visiting card fortunately mentioned the designation of a Director and that probably made an impact. She picked up her phone and dialled the intercom. My mind started racing as to how we were going to introduce ourselves. How do we make sure he gave us five minutes of his time. Mr. Anonymous, as a name drop, will certainly not help. The moment was here, the receptionist was holding out the phone to me.

I was blank, just then I thought to blabber out the truth. I took the phone, started with a greeting, "Good morning, sir. I found an Urdu Manuscript on *Trigunas – Sattva*, *Rajas* and *Tamas*, written by the boss at the library in Connaught Place. Sir, my wife and I have assimilated and are implementing each word that he has written. Can you please give us five minutes of your time?" My heart was skipping a beat, it was a make or break moment to meet Mr. Anonymous.

There was a moment of silence as though Mr. Pahwa was going down a memory lane. We did not even know whether we were at the right place or whether Mr. Anonymous was still alive or not. Finally the silence broke and the husky old voice on the other side said, "Give the phone to the lady, please." So I did. After a short conversation the lady asked us to take a seat and called for an escort to take us in. We cheered! Neha said excitedly, "We seem to be at the right place!"

Dutiful men never retire; they merely change their roles.

CHAPTER NINETEEN

HIMAAYAT ALI

A young man escorted us to the lift and took us to the 14th floor in tower 3. The entry to the floor was plush and clearly announced that this floor was the boss's office. There was another reception at this floor with luxuriant sofas and the office help on this floor were wearing bows and white gloves. We were taken straight in and finally reached a rich mahogany door. Our escort knocked and indicated us to go in. An old man with loose salt and pepper hair was sitting on the sofa. The cabin was big with a conventional chair and table set up and a small sitting area with a coffee table.

I sprung my hand forward and muttered, "Mr. Vijender Pahwa," to which he nodded his head. I introduced my wife and myself. I thanked him for his time and explained to him how we had found the handwritten Urdu manuscript and got influenced by his philosophies. Neha told him how the fortunate finding had changed our lives for the better. She said, "The clarity of thought is helping in our work and personal life. We have been addressing the writer as Mr. Anonymous and cannot thank him enough for his teachings."

In heart of heart we were both waiting to hear from Mr. Pahwa that Mr. Anonymous was still around and we would be able to take his blessings. Mr. Pahwa finally spoke,

"Boss has been our friend, philosopher and guide. We as a team still live by his philosophies. There comes a point in one's life when there is an urge to share everything. I think boss reached that point at the time of writing this bunch, which we published in our in-house magazine." Neha and I were trying to analyse every word and hoping to get a hint as to where Mr. Anonymous was.

Mr. Pahwa continued, "He wrote this beautiful piece after running this company through professional hands for a few years and exited when he was satisfied that he had chosen the right professionals for the job. His family still owns a substantial stake. He has two daughters who are happily married. His cousins now hold the rest of the stake in the company. I have been fortunate to serve as his secretary for 28 years and continue to do so."

I could see the expression of relief on Neha's face. We were sitting in front of the right man and Mr. Anonymous was very much still alive to extend his teachings. It was too early to pop the question of meeting him. The risk of losing our chance to meet him was way too much. He extended the gesture of tea, coffee or plain milk. I, being a salesperson, sensed an opportunity to buy more time and quickly accepted the gesture and said, "Hot milk."

Neha quizzed, "When was this bunch written?"

Mr. Pahwa replied, "Nine years ago, just before Boss announced his retirement. I thought of leaving the company with him and join his trust but was urged by the rest to remain here as a guiding light. The management has given me so much respect and often ask me as to what would Boss have done at a particular juncture. I have worked with Boss for 28 years and have seen him nurture this organisation from a 500 square feet office in Nehru Place to its present stature."

Neha tried her luck, "Where is he now? What does he do?"

Mr. Pahwa responded with pride, "Boss runs a trust called Nishkaam Nishtha that works in the field of education at all levels. He runs nurturing centres for poor children and also gives college scholarships for the underprivileged. Have you heard of the start up laboratory concept in Gurgaon?"

I suddenly remembered to have read about this facility where aspiring entrepreneurs could present their idea. If chosen, he would be given infrastructure and financial support to build his own company. I read about it in an article that spoke about innovative ways of inculcating philanthropy. If the idea succeeds it would have to give 2 percent of its profits to Nishkaam Nishtha while the complete ownership would remain with its founder.

The hot milk was served and we got more time to put forth our request for an appointment. After some more conversation, I requested him to please get us an appointment. He said, "Boss will surely give you an appointment as he had personally kept the Urdu manuscript back in the library for this very purpose. After publication I advised him to keep the hand written original manuscript at a place where fate would take it to the one who deserves it. He will be glad to know it reached the right hands."

"Wow, that was very thoughtful, lucky us!" Neha exclaimed.

Mr. Pahwa picked up his Airmax mobile phone and dialled Mr. Anonymous. He stood up from his seat as he greeted Mr. Anonymous and informed him of our visit. It seemed Mr. Anonymous asked Mr. Pahwa to escort us to his dwelling. Mr. Pahwa asked for his car to take us to him. We were delighted. After spending months reading and treading on the philosophies of Mr. Anonymous, we were about to meet him.

On the way Mr. Pahwa told us about the simple ways in which Boss lived. "Boss has read all the scriptures and regards each one as a philosophy of living and does not attach it to any of the religions. He treats the Glorious Quran, the Holy Bible and the Bhagavad Gita, all, as his source of wisdom. He has detached the rituals from religions and delves into the philosophy and scriptures of all. After a brisk walk and Yoga in the morning he spends an hour reading philosophy in the scriptures. Thereafter he works by the minute till evening even at this age."

As the car turned into the driveway, we crossed a neatly manicured garden with pleasing flowers to the right. On the left was a house and a separate office structure. We stopped next to the office building and walked into the reception. It was unmanned and had a hand-painted life-sized depiction of the scene from the Mahabharat in which Shri Krishna imparts the knowledge of Gita to Arjuna on the chariot in the battlefield.

Mr. Pahwha showed us the way into an alley. On the way we saw a room labeled as 'Hermitage' and ten steps ahead we entered a office. Finally, here we were, right in front of an extremely successful man who lived by a philosophy.

As expected Mr. Anonymous was in his late seventies, he had wheatish skin colour and loose white hair. He got up and walked to the sitting area to greet us. He walked with firm steps and a straight spine, which was commendable for a man his age. He was dressed in a black pants and a light shirt like any other corporate executive. He greeted us with a handshake and gestured, "Glad to meet you."

We responded from our heart, "Sir, it is an honour to meet you."

We told him how we found the Urdu Manuscript on the *Trigunas* and also expressed our gratitude as to how it has been instrumental in living a better quality of life. To which, he exclaimed "Oh that one!" Neha and I shared a glance acknowledging the existence of more such manuscripts in the library.

Neha could not control her curiosity and popped a question straight on, "Sir, what do you mean by saying 'that one'?"

He said, "I guess you found the manuscript in the shelves that contain books of Shri Adi Shankaracharya in the library." I nodded in affirmation as I recollected. He continued, "I research wisdom free of religion. My company has a majority of Hindus. My purpose was to give them wisdom that they can implement in their lives and not to convert their religion, although I did write a similar write-up with extracts from the Holy Quran also. I left that manuscript in the shelves containing books on Islam."

"I have researched many scriptures and found that a substantial part of the scriptures talk about the cycle of life and death and also freedom from the cycle of life and death. And a substantial part of the scriptures also talks about life here and now, the law of *Karma*, how to reduce your suffering and seek everlasting happiness in this very life."

"Although I know that until Galileo discovered that the earth was round everybody thought it was flat. I made a choice, I did not want to be Galileo and discover the unknown. I researched various philosophies across all religions to assimilate how to live a better quality of life here and now."

"Our scripture acknowledges all lifestyles with equal respect. It talks about living a life with the sole purpose to fulfill ones desires with as much reverence as living a dutiful life of austerities. The *Vidya* of fulfilling desires is termed as *Kamya Vidya* and the *Vidya* of dutiful life of austerities is called *Kartavya Vidya*. At all these junctions I made my choice with a sole motive. I was clear in my mind that I wanted to research a life of pursuing excellence in my duty. I wanted to research and experience my findings. I have lived more than half a century with conscious nurturing of *Trigunas*. I have experienced the pros and cons of various philosophies and only then tried to pass on my learnings."

"Sir, can you clarify with an example as to why you say our scriptures acknowledge all lifestyles with equal respect?" I asked.

He replied with a popular example. "Although alcohol is *Tamasik*, our philosophies are so inclusive that they even talk about *Rajasik style* of drinking alcohol. Drinking alcohol to a point of losing focus is *Tamasik*. Drinking alcohol and boasting or flaunting one's possessions is *Rajasik*. Although alcohol drains energy, slow and limited consumption acts as a stimulant in nurturing a thought. The biggest issue with intoxicants is that the desire to consume more quantity is inadvertent. With consumption of intoxicants, one is prone to slip from one's path."

Mr. Pahwa put forth a query too, "Sir, I have noticed that your attire never reflects any religion but I have also noticed that you wear a thread over your shoulder much like the *Janeau* worn by many Hindu communities." It seemed that Mr. Pahwa had noticed the thread over the years but had never found the courage to ask.

Mr. Anonymous replied, "Reflecting one's philosophy in one's attire is following rituals and has nothing to do with the essence of the philosophy. Rituals are made in a religion to reiterate its philosophies. Any externalisation helps in reiteration of a feeling just like standing in front of an idol of god gives the feeling of serenity within. The flip side of this externalisation via rituals is that it cultivates polarisation and communal living, which is bad for humanity at large.

"I have had my share of slips from my path. I realised that some kind of reiteration was required. At the same time, I did not want it to show as a part of my attire. So I wore a thread over my shoulder as my way of reiteration."

We told Mr. Anonymous about our experiences of living by the philosophy of *Trigunas*. I expressed how *Trigunas* had an effect on the management and success of our company. He reiterated the same by acknowledging the effect of the concept of *Trigunas* on his management style too.

My sight fell on the name etched on the diary that Mr. Anonymous was carrying and was taken aback as I read the name on it. I did not know whether Neha had noticed the same. Perhaps Mr. Anonymous was carrying somebody else's diary. I looked at his attire carefully to find out his religion.

I looked at the walls for a clue. I could see the Gita, Quran, Bible, Guru Granth Sahib all on his bookshelf. I was frantically looking for a sign.

His name as mentioned on the diary was 'Himaayat Ali'.

Rituals and attire are made to reiterate the philosophies in a religion, the flip side being that they tend to cultivate polarisation.

AUTHOR'S NOTE

The beginning of this journey has been interesting and satisfactory. The slips have been an integral part of the journey. I just hope and pray the track that unfolds over time, gives me the courage and discipline to 'keep walking' (Black Label; pun intended).

I like to steal light moments periodically and contribute substantially in planning fun activities. I know my compilation does not back my claim to comedy. Discipline tends to make more serious moments than lighter ones but it is up to us to create the lighter ones from time to time.

I now prefer eating vegetarian, though I have kept the door open by allowing myself to eat fish and even have an alcoholic drink, in a business meeting. Although, indulgence in both is very rare.

Life will definitely move on with time. Evenings can be action-packed with delicious food and drinks. Years and decades can be lived with fun and phases of unexpected sadness. The thrill, excitement, fun, sadness, are all bound to unveil. Life is sure to move on and reach its biological end. I often ask myself, *Is that it? 80-100 years of my life!*

I don't know how, when and why the thought of 'pursuing excellence in this lifetime' sprouted in me. My mind was set to excel in philosophy and spirituality, reading and writing being complementary activities. I thought to myself that excellence at work will be an offshoot of clarity of mind. I decided to cut down on all other indulgences such as sports, movies, eating out, etc. I wanted to do more than just living and reaching the end of this lifetime. I wanted to pursue excellence in some field. I started to give reading and writing more focused time.

So here I am, in solitude within the bustling city, in pursuit; in pursuit of Self, in pursuit of Knowledge, in pursuit of Writing, in pursuit of Excellence. I discovered happiness; in pursuit of excellence with detachment from its fruit. Pursuit with detachment can be everlasting and eternal, so can be state of happiness.

Although I was hesitant, my editor insisted I mention the changes that I felt in my life and also how the changes manifested in the real world. Firstly, I must acknowledge reduced emotions of anger, excitement or tension. The slips have been a part of my life and I respect these deteriorated phases as teaching in disguise.

On the way till now, I have picked up the skill of playing the keyboard, which I started learning a couple of years back. Our company's turnover has grown four times in the last four years, it has been a team effort. I stay in a joint family of ten and feel blessed in the arrangement. I realised that if the feeling of love, empathy and compassion can be nurtured within ten people, it makes life heavenly. And if the same feeling of love, empathy and compassion can be nurtured within everybody, it will create heaven on earth.

Most part of this compilation is non-fiction. Writing has been a pursuit since my stint as a content writer in the *Times Of India* group. My articles have been printed in both *Times of India* and *Economic Times*. After many years in business, I

Author's Note

got into reading scriptures. The library helped me venture into philosophies I was unaware of. When I started writing I had no idea it would end up as a book. After a couple of years of writing I decided to weave the thought provoking notes into a readable fiction and the rest just happened.

I have already expressed my gratitude in the beginning of the book and I am inclined reiterate it again. Thank you Almighty, Thank you Shri Krishna. I also thank my friends and family for their support. I consider starting and finishing this book as a milestone in my life, which would not have been possible without imbibing this new lifestyle.

The purpose of my compilation is two fold.

The nonfiction part is a belief that if at all the theory of rebirth is true, I have faith that in my next birth the universe will lead me to these compilations to evolve my manifestation further.

The fiction part is an attempt to make the compilation appealing to readers.

I thank you for taking out time to read this compilation and hope it adds value to your life also.

For corporate training or interactive session on the subject please write to nishkaamnishtha@gmail.com. Please follow us on Twitter @M_CityHermit and on Facebook at www.facebook.com/The-Millennium-City-Hermit-287672304897798

RESEARCH WORK

Authors and Year	Summary	Strength	Limitations
Mallikarjun, 2004 (M.Sc. Dissertation)	*Explained the concept of Triguna and Tridosa to elucidate the holistic health concept and nature of psychosomatic diseases.*	Comparisons of *Ayurveda* and Yoga concepts. Comprehensive approach towards holistic health. Highlights the use of *triguna* and *tridosa* for complete ascertainment of individual nature.	No theoretical model. Experimental work different from literary search.
Mohan, 2008 (M.Sc. Dissertation)	*Highlighted challenges due to modern lifestyle, and their influence in attitude formation.* *Triguna concept presented to suggest methods to overcome poor lifestyle and develop a better attitude towards life.*	Presentation of *Triguna* concept from practical perspective of lifestyle management.	No theoretical model. Experimental work different from literary search.
Tripathi, 2012 (M.Sc. Dissertation)	*A detailed comparison is made between Yoga and Ayurveda in understanding the concept of Triguna.*	Parallels and contrasts in *Triguna* according to Yoga and Ayurveda texts. Major ayurvedic texts and yoga texts were referred	No theoretical model was proposed related to experimental work. Experimental work different from literary search

Continued

Authors and Year	Summary	Strength	Limitations
Rao, 2013 (M.Sc. Dissertation)	Attempted a novel method to understand the basic equilibrium pattern in the Prakriti, the universe.* Randomness in nature due to human interaction (Guna flux) was studied using the Random Event Generator (REG)	Concise review of relevant verses needed to support theoretical ideas. New application of *Triguna* theory Theoretical frameworks proposed related to experimental work. Introduction of the concept of *gunagraphy*	Major focus on study of *Gunas* in inanimate *Prakriti* (i.e. external environment)
Deshpande, 2008 (Ph.D. Theses)	Quality of life was studied from various dimensions, having Triguna as one of the main components of study.	Used *Triguna* as the major tool for assessing personality Extensive review from major *Upanishads*, Yoga and *Ayurveda* texts	Major focus on quality of life, *Triguna* being a part of the whole study. No theoretical model proposed related to experimental work.
Khemka, 2012 (Ph.D. Thesis)	The study of development of human potential through practice of Yoga and assessment of the changes using psychological and health variables.	Theoretical model proposed for development of human potential.	Major focus on human potential model, *Triguna* being a part of the whole study.

This particular work done by Dr. Judu to design an implicit tool to know the present proportion of *Gunas* in a person caught my interest. There are tools already made to know the proportion of *Gunas* but having the knowledge of *Gunas* may lead one to manipulate the inputs to have a desired result. So Dr. Judu made a new tool where such manipulation of the subconscious mind can also be avoided and that tool is described as an implicit tool.

Some of the tools to test the proportion of *Gunas* in a person are listed below with examples of the result format.

1. *Guna* – **Implicit Association Test (G-IAT):** A reaction time task.

G-I AT

Guna (Implicit)	Your Score
Sattva	**-23.28001**
Rajas	**97.68007**
Tamas	**-14.46001**

Interpretation of G-IAT scores: The range of score is from -600 to +600 millisecond. The more positive score you get, the more you evaluate yourself to be *Sattvik* implicitly, i.e., within. Negative score means you do not evaluate yourself to be *Sattvik* implicitly, i.e., within. A score of 0 means you do not have special preference towards either side. For example, a score of +230 means **I** consider myself *very Sattvik* inherently. A score of -50 would mean **I** consider myself slightly *not Sattvik*. Similarly, the scores of *Rajas* and *Tamas* are evaluated.

2. **Feeling Thermometer (FT):** A 10-point self-rating scale to evaluate your *Guna*.

Feeling Thermometer scores:

Guna (Explicit)	Your- Score
Sattva	5
Rajas	4
Tamas	-14.46001

This is how much you rate yourself to be *Sattvik*, *Rajasik*, and *Tamasik* on a 10-point visual analog scale. A positive score means you consider yourself to be more *Sattvik*, a negative score means you consider yourself to be not *Sattvik*, a score of 0 means you consider yourself to be moderately *Sattvik*. Similarly, the scores of *Rajas* and *Tamas* are interpreted.

3. **Vedic Personality Inventory (VPI):** A 56-question questionnaire to assess *Gunas*. This is to correlate with *Sattva* scores of a person.

Vedic Personality Inventory (VPI):

Guna Percentage (Explicit)	Your Score
Sattva	35.869999999999997
Rajas	31.25
Tamas	32.890000000000001

VPI has 56 questions. It gives an estimate of your *Sattva*, *Rajas*, and *Tamas* as reported by you. The scores are given as percentages, e.g., 30% *Tamas*, 40% *Rajas*, and 30% *Sattva*, etc. For each *Guna* your score may vary from 0 to 100 %.

Another Interesting research done by Mr. Sudheer Deshpande was on the 'Influence of Yoga on Quality of Life'.

This research work measured the effect of Yoga compared to the effect of Physical Exercise on the *Gunas* of the person. He used another popular tool to measure the portion of *Gunas* in a person called 'The 'G' Inventory of personality.' I pulled out some extracts from the research, which were relevant to the *Gunas*.

The aggregated 184 people were divided randomly into 2 groups and their *Gunas* were measured. One group practiced Yoga for 8 weeks and the other was involved in physical exercise for 8 weeks. After 8 weeks, again their set of *Gunas* were measured. The finding of the same is mentioned below.

DEMOGRAPHY

The table below shows the demographic data. There were 92 females and 92 males within the age range of 18–71 years. The mean age was approximately 30 years. They belonged to different callings. There were 85 college students, 50 employees, 29 housewives, 11 business people and nine professionals. The subjects were selected from five different areas of Bangalore (North, South, East, West and Central).

Demographic Data of subjects

	Yoga	**P.E.**
No. of Participants (n)	92	92
Avg. Age (years)	29.73 (12.38)	30.26 (12.29)
Range	18-71	18-60

Continued

	Yoga	P.E.
Gender		
Females	42	39
Males	50	53
Students	45	40
Employees	20	30
Housewives	20	30
Businessmen	8	3
Professionals	9	

Improvement in *Gunas* in "The 'G" — Inventory of Personality"

	Yoga		Physical Exercise	
Personality				
	Pre	Post	Pre	Post
Sattva	8	17	5	9
Rajas	54	57	60	62
Tamas	25	13	22	16

Figure: Improvement in *Gunas* in Yoga, Physical Exercise

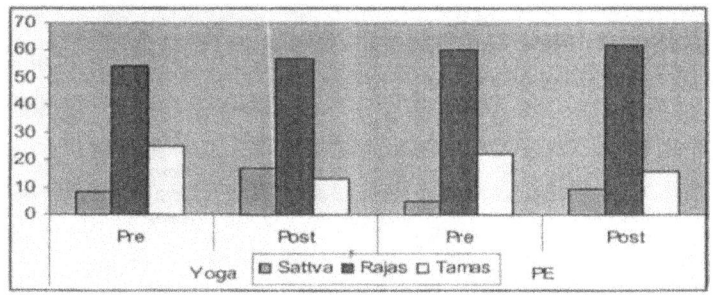

In the Yoga group, *Sattva* and *Rajas* participants have increased whereas *Tamas* participants have decreased.

In Physical Exercise group also the same trend was noticed.

4. "The 'G' Inventory of Personality"

This has 10 questions to evaluate *Tamas, Rajas* and *Sattva Gunas*. The score value of weightage of an item indicating *Sattva* is 3, for an item indicating *Rajas* is 2, and for an item indicating *Tamas* is 1. It classifies people as being predominantly of *Sattva, Rajas* or *Tamas* type depending on their total score on the test.